A THOUSAND CAMELS FOR YOUR GAZELLE
Narratives and Psychiatry

DANIEL ROSEN

A THOUSAND CAMELS
FOR YOUR GAZELLE
Narratives and Psychiatry

Translations from French by the author

IPBOOKS.net
International Psychoanalytic Books

International Psychoanalytic Books (IPBooks)
New York • https://ipbooks.net

All persons and events in this book are fictional. Any resemblance to any actual persons, living or dead, or events, past, present or future is purely coincidental.

International Psychoanalytic Books (IPBooks)
Queens, NY 11102
Online at: https://ipbooks.net

Illustrations:
Front cover: *Triangles,* painting by Daniel Rosen, 1993
Page 16: *Meurtrière (Murder-Hole),* photo by Daniel Rosen, 2019
Page 46: *Chénsī de (Pensive),* photo by Daniel Rosen, 1993
Page 205: *Triangles and Squares,* photo by Daniel Rosen, 1993
Between the chapters: *Triangles Variations*, by Daniel Rosen, 2021

ISBN: 978-1-949093-90-2

CONTENTS

i

iii

Chapters about Narrative in Psychiatry: 7, 8, 9, 12, and 22.

Foreword

The stories collected here are not just about relationships. They are themselves what form and inform these relationships. Stories can sometimes be all that we have left to bring the past into connection with the present in ways that make a future possible. The stories in this book were written during the first year of the Corona virus pandemic. Though the pandemic is often in the background, it only plays a part, directly or indirectly, in a handful of the stories, including one written in the form of an essay on the use of fictional narratives as a coping mechanism. Narratives, autobiographical or imagined can help as a therapeutic tool to prepare for an anticipated trauma, and integrate previously fragmented responses to traumatic experiences. Storytelling can foster connections by providing narrators with testimonies which can be witnessed and shared.

Many of the various stories presented here are reflections on relationships, from engaging in a new one, to mourning a lost one, or sharing a happy or sad experience, or trying to master and anticipate these experiences. These stories were gathered and, after meeting in this collection, they started communicating with each other without any authorial control, like a Golem living its own life after escaping from his creator's grasp.

As in *Butterfly Words*,[1] I am again so grateful to William S. Cohen for catching these internal conversations and disclosing meanings and connections I had not been able to grasp and even still cannot fathom. His insights are recorded

---

[1] See William S. Cohen introduction of my previous book: *Butterfly Words: Relationships, A Psychiatrist's Narrative. International Psychoanalytic Books, New York, NY. 2019.*

1

in the afterword. I have been asked: "Who is this William S. Cohen who seems to know you so well?" Yes, he has been with me all these years, a devoted observer, sometimes detached, sometimes ironic, analyzing the writings as a critic looks into a foreign text.

I thank my teachers and my colleagues and all the voluntary and involuntary participants or recipients of those stories. But above all, I thank my patients for sharing their lives with me and also for their teaching. I am thinking for example of a former patient hospitalized in a psychiatric ward for a chronic mental illness. He was homeless, jobless, with no money, no family or friends. He was not demented but had some cognitive impairment. He was able to walk but was unsteady on his feet. Once he got better, he said with a smile that he wanted to leave the hospital and go back to the shelter and "work." What was his work? To collect empty cans of soda for recycling. "People give me money when they see me do that." That was his job. I was amazed: How could he be in such good spirits when he had less than nothing? I am grateful for that lesson of life.

I am also grateful to the following clinicians who provided helpful comments and feedback upon the manuscript of chapters 7, 8 and 9: Mark J. Russ, M.D. and Michael B. Klein, Ph.D. I also wish to thank Matthew Bach for his close reading of the entire manuscript and for his insightful editorial comments.

I thank all those who inspired me, as I thank the muses, the amused muses who played with me and wrote these words.

Daniel Rosen

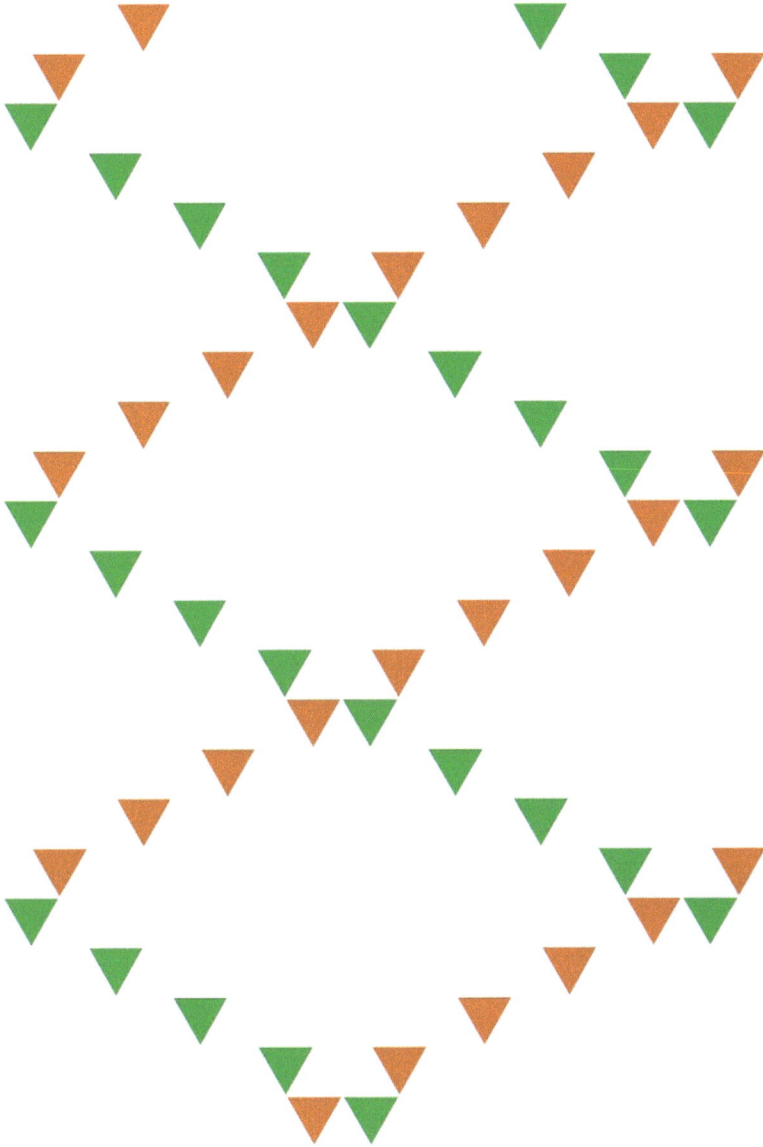

1 The Day after the Plague

Before

Before I tell you what happened the day after they decided that we could finally leave our home and that the plague was now controlled, let me explain what it's like to have divorced parents. When a few years ago they told us that they were getting divorced, my first reaction was that it will be great to have two rooms for me instead of just one. Boy was I wrong. I ended up hating the back and forth, and tried to bargain my way out of that arrangement. But there was something I did not think about then, which did come out great. Being between them, I could get away with things more easily. They both try to be nice to me, and they can be a bit annoying about that. They both have a great opinion of me, and that also can be annoying. Especially my dad. He keeps telling that story from when I was in first grade. I'll tell it to you, just to get it over with.

One day in first grade, the school had arranged for a parent to talk to us about her job for an hour. This mother who came was doing developmental neuro-embryology, or something like that. She talked to us about the neural tube and the different areas of the brain, sensory and motor areas. I thought nothing of it. But a few months later, that mom came to our home and reported the question I had asked at the end of her talk:

"Does the mind command the brain? Otherwise there wouldn't be any free will!"

My dad went nuts about this one thing I said. It's not like we had discussions about free will at the dining room table. He must have thought that I was an Einstein or something. This was before I went through the phase when I thought that everything we do was predetermined from the Big Bang on. Pretty stupid – right?

There is one more story my dad likes to tell a lot. I must have been between 2 and 3. My dad has this thing that he wants us to learn fucking languages, excuse my French. So he insisted that we alternate videos: one day in English, one day in a foreign language. I told you he was annoying. And they would limit the number of hours I could watch videos. That was back then. Now, I don't let them limit anything. And there is nothing they can do about it. Anyway, it was Friday afternoon and I had already watched my quota of TV. Friday afternoon is usually a busy time preparing for Shabbat, in order to be ready on time for lighting candles. But, as always, I still wanted to watch more TV. So, while everyone was running around, I told them:

"Make it easy on yourself, let me watch TV!"

They both laughed because of my age. Okay, it was funny, I admit. So they put a tape in the tape player and let me watch it. Eh, I am not a dinosaur, OK! They had tape players back then. When the tape started, I told them:

"You see, it's in French. That will make YOU happy!"

They are still cracking up, telling that story.

I had to work very hard to lower their expectations. My goal was to be just above mediocre. You know, so that they wouldn't think I would work my ass off and end up at Harvard or MIT – see? I tried to lower my grades in Jewish Studies, but the guy would still give me an OK grade, despite me not doing much homework. I would usually compensate by saying a few words of wisdom in class. I even asked to be switched from my Jewish school with its extra-long curriculum to a public school where I could leave by 2 instead of 5. And when I got to that public school, I started to work a little more to get some decent grades, just to keep them off my back. But I didn't work too hard, so I wouldn't have to go to a high-pressure Ivy League school. In any case, with the divorce, money was tight and I was aiming to go to a local State school or go somewhere on a basketball scholarship.

I used the basketball thing to keep mom and dad off my back. The second year in the new school I got kicked off the team. Not really kicked off it. The coach just didn't pick me. Which was surprising, because I am the tallest in my grade, and the second tallest of the entire school, and I am a decent player. I got two things from my grandpa: his height, and his great Texas style hat. When my father kicked me out of his house, I took just a few things, including that hat. Now that I am back, I did put the hat back in my room here. Anyway, my parents had me go to therapy so I would agree to go back to dad's every other week after he kicked me out. My mom insisted that I come to the session on the evening when the coach selected the new team in the beginning of the year. My dad even came to get me at school with his car, for us to be on time. After I learned that I did not make it onto the team, I told my parents that I wasn't picked because I had to leave early that evening to go to that therapy meeting, so the coach didn't have a chance to see how good I was. They didn't blame each other for it, but they were pretty upset because they knew how much I loved playing basketball with my friends, and at school. My mom tried to downplay the whole thing, but I could sense that my dad felt guilty about it. I got a lot of positive attention from that.

The truth? My grades were not good enough for the first year in that public school, and they had a policy that you had to have a certain grade in order to make the team.

During

During the plague, my parents cooperated surprisingly well; although I was not worried that they would get back together. They bounced us between their homes like a bunch of hot potatoes. However, each time it was to protect the family. Once, despite wanting us to stay, my dad sent us back to mom, because he was afraid that he may have gotten the plague.

After a week, it turned out to be a false alarm, but by then it was mom's turn to have symptoms and to be concerned about having been infected. We all decided that it was better for us to stay at mom's. She decided to cloister herself in her bedroom, rather than us going to dad and risking contaminating him from her illness. Although by staying at mom's, we were taking some risk of getting it from her despite her isolation because we had only one shared bathroom. But since we were young it was less risky than for dad who, of course, was older.

My sister and I took good care of mom, doing the laundry and preparing her food since she did not have access to the kitchen. My sister even made a simple version of a beef Bourguignon! Mom had asked my dad before if we could stay with him this weekend, because she needed some rest after all the work she did helping control the plague, but now she kept us by her for his sake. That is the kind of generous person my mom is. OK, maybe she kept us because she did not want to hear my dad freaking out if he got infected. But still, it was at least thoughtful. Funny how it worked out that in a time of stress, we were all trying to take care of each other. My dad used to say:

"When we pray for *shalom bayit*, (peace in the home), this applies also to a broken home. Even a broken home needs peace."

Of course, in a literal sense it is absurd to say that a broken home needs *shalom bayit*. *Shalom bayit* means to prevent a broken home. He is like that, my dad. When I talk to him, I call him "bro." He does not mind too much, but the therapist doesn't like it. But he is right, bro, even a broken home needs some peace.

After

On the day after the plague, it was like we were all in a dream. I could go back to school, finally. A few days before it closed, my dad had asked me if I wanted to stay out of school, to avoid being infected. I told him that he and mom couldn't keep me from going to school and that, if it was open, I would go. I think my dad was surprised to hear that. He must have thought I was lazy or something.

I was happy to see my friends for real instead of Zooming all the time. I really got sick of Zoom after a while. And now I could go to a court in the park and play pickup basketball. This is when you play with people you just meet in the park. It is also nice to see some girls. I must tell you, I have game. With girls, I mean. Because of my height, I look much older than my age, and girls like that.

Everyone is now crazy about nature and picnics and hiking and biking, especially since the weather has gotten real nice. One summer, my father had us hike in the Alps in cow poop while it was raining, going around the White Mountain. "Le Tour du Mont Blanc" it was called. I hate hiking. I hate biking. I hate nature. I hate traveling. I hate wine. I hate gourmet meals. I hate talking to adults. They have a warped idea of a good time. During the plague, it was good. I could stay in my room with my computer and play video games while I was hurrying through my homework, and nobody would say anything but "Oh the pauvre chéri, he is confined." "Pauvre chéri" means "(poor) little darling." I don't mind throwing in a few of the French words I learned from the video I watched on that Friday afternoon when I was not yet three.

12

Confined meant that you could stay in bed late, and play on the computer all night. Initially they hadn't figured out classes, so all we had to do was some homework. It was good, bro. It was good.

It was good, OK. But I also enjoyed when it ended. Not because I missed seeing butterflies, I couldn't care less. But my eyes were getting pretty tired of looking only at that computer screen. And also, I needed a haircut. But mostly to connect with my friends – for real. Some families were hit hard; some like us were hardly hit. Sorry, I was not trying to make a pun when talking about that. In our school, kids were mostly of the nerd type, so before the plague they would talk, but not too much. Only the Chinese kids would talk a lot in freaking Chinese, among themselves.

Now things are different. Everyone is asking about everybody, and especially about those who are not here. We don't have the right to visit the few in the hospital, but we try to talk to their family.

Some of the kids who were living in shelters ended up finally in hotels in order to enforce "social distancing," as they said. I think my mom was working to arrange that, or she had colleagues working on that. Some of our teachers got sick, and we sent them cards.

One fall day last year, while walking in Midtown, I suddenly heard the blast of machine gun fire. Everyone ran for cover, crouching down behind parked cars. We all slowly realized the noise had come from a big truck – from a broken transmission belt or something. After we stood up, everyone started talking with each other for support, being there for each other after the chilling moment we had all just been through. In Midtown, all these strangers – talking!

It is a little like that in our school now, except that this time there was no broken truck and it was not a video game. It was for real.

New York, March 29, 2020

2 La Meurtrière de Lumière
The Murder-Hole of Light

Original in French   17-18
English translation   19-20

Pages 18 and 20: *Cross on Via Dolorosa*, drawing by Daniel Rosen, 2020

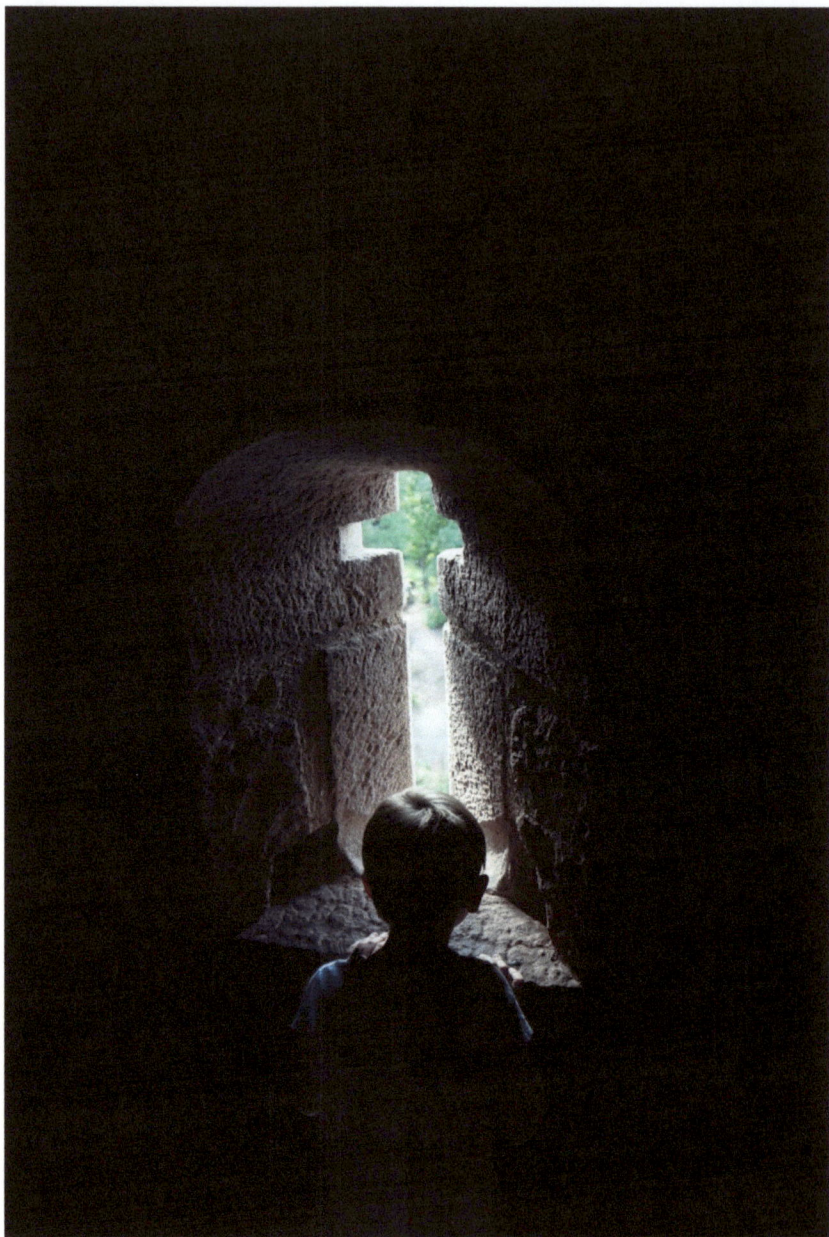

Meurtrière (Murder-Hole), Château du Haut-Kœnigsbourg, France.
Daniel Rosen, July 2019.

16

La Meurtrière de Lumière

Croix de lumière
Croix d'espoir
Un enfant dans le noir regarde la lumière
A travers l'épaisse muraille
A travers la meurtrière
Jadis utilisée pour tuer
Maintenant offrant une vue paisible
Au-delà de l'isolation
Au-delà de la mort rampante
A l'intérieur des remparts

"Dominus vobiscum"
"The Lord be with you"
Mais qui répondrait ?
"Et cum spiritu tuo."
"And with Thy spirit."
A qui prêchait-il ?
A des confinés
A qui dispensait-il l'absolution ?
A qui donnerait-il l'hostie ?
A une caméra vidéo.
Une messe confidentielle
Dans une église confinentielle

*"Commixtio salis et aquæ pariter fiat in nomine Patris, et Filii et
Spiritus Sancti."*
*"May a mixture of salt and water now be made in the name of the
Father, and of the Son, and of the Holy Spirit."*
Mon Dieu, mon Dieu
Eli, Eli,
Pourquoi m'as-tu abandonné ?
Lama Sabachthani ?
Son église vide pendant la Semaine Sainte !

Mais avait-on maintenant besoin d'une église
Pour reconstituer la Passion du Christ
Pour pouvoir communier
Avec la souffrance de l'Esprit Saint ?

"Confíteor Deo omnipoténti"
"I confess to almighty God"
La Via Dolorosa maintenant désertée.
Lors de sa visite à la Ville Sainte
Il se rappelait des pèlerins
Portant la lourde croix de bois
Imitant le Christ dans son Calvaire.
Un pèlerin en soutane avait ajouté deux petites roues
Au bas de la croix
Pour alléger le fardeau.
Humaine contradiction, voulant re-expérimenter
La Divine souffrance,
Mais pas trop.

"Introibo ad altare Dei, ad Deum qui lætificat iuventutem meam"
"I shall go in to the altar of God: to God who giveth joy to my youth"
Oh Notre Père
Allège notre fléau.
Agnus Dei, Agneau de Dieu,
Qui enlève les péchés du monde
Aie pitié de nous.

Donne-nous deux petites roues
Pour nous aider
A supporter Ta croix

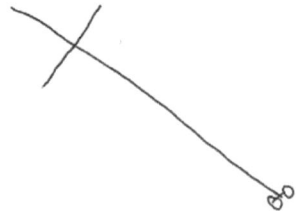

New York, le lundi 6 avril 2020
Pendant la Semaine Sainte

18

The Murder-Hole of Light

Cross of light
Cross of hope
A boy in the dark looks at the light
Through the thick wall
Through the murder-hole
Once used to kill
Now offering a peaceful view
Beyond the isolation
Beyond the rampant death
Inside the ramparts

Dominus vobiscum
The Lord be with you
But who would answer?
Et cum spiritu tuo.
And with Thy spirit.
To whom was he preaching?
To a confined flock.
To whom was he granting absolution?
To whom would he give the communion wafer?
To a video camera.
A confidential mass
In a confinential Church.

Commixtio salis et aquæ pariter fiat in nomine Patris, et Filii et
Spiritus Sancti.
May a mixture of salt and water now be made in the name of the
Father, and of the Son, and of the Holy Spirit.
My God, my God
Eli, Eli,
Why did you abandon me?
Lama Sabachthani?
His church empty during the Holy Week!

19

But did we now need a church
To reenact the Passion of Christ
To be able to unite
With the suffering of the Holy Spirit?

Confíteor Deo omnipoténti
I confess to almighty God
The Via Dolorosa now deserted.
During his visit to the Holy City
He remembered the pilgrims
Carrying the heavy wooden cross
Imitating the Christ in his Calvary.
One pilgrim in his robe added two small wheels
At the bottom of the cross
To lighten the load.
Human contradiction, trying to re-experience
The Divine suffering,
But not too much.

Introibo ad altare Dei, ad Deum qui lætificat iuventutem meam
I shall go in to the altar of God: to God who giveth joy to my youth
Oh Our Father
Ease our plague.
Agnus Dei, Lamb of God,
Who removes the sins of the world,
Have mercy on us.

Give us two small wheels
To help us
Carry Your cross

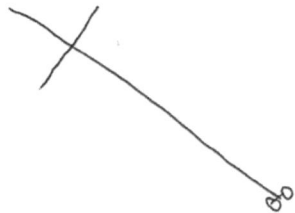

New York, Monday March April 6, 2020
During the Holy Week.
Translated from French.

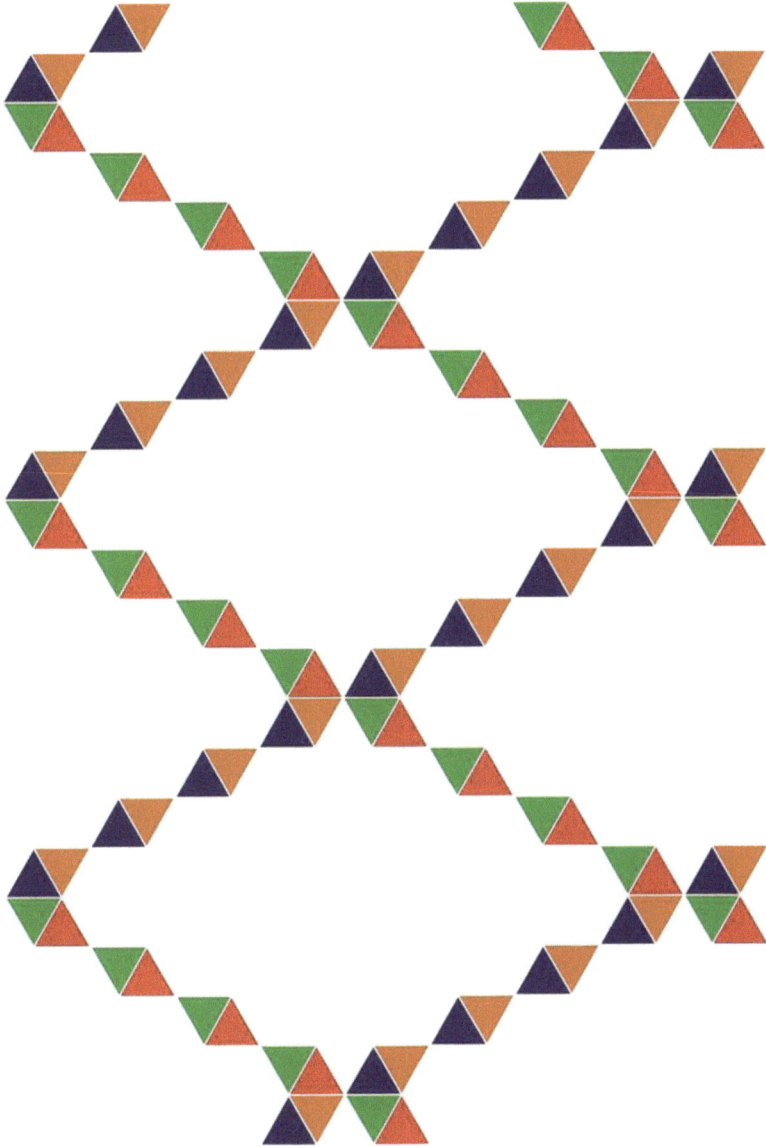

3 Morning Blessing

Like fresh ink spots on blotting paper, the borders of words, for Dani were fuzzy, spreading their coronated radicles, their definitions blurring, their meanings merging.

As a foreign autodidact, grammar was a mystery (should one say "Must have forgot" or "Must have forgotten"?), and so was pronunciation and spelling. Why was the g in "gym" soft, while it was hard in "gum"? Why was the pronunciation of "oo" in "flood" and in "food" so different?

And what about the "i" in "Gina" pronounced Geena, (this time autocorrect was wrong, the isolated "i" with its ominous red line under it would stay uncapitalized—another red line: is *uncapitalized* a word?—) while the "i" of vagina was pronounced like "eye." Why?

Meanings also were fuzzy, leaving traces crossing languages like souvenirs collecting dust. The resonance of those souvenirs added layers of associations which could be decoded only if you also knew the other language, for example, the ink spot "souvenir" and the ink spot "memory" overlapped in one language but not in the other.[i] When a third language was added, the fuzziness thickened.

In this time of Corona and social distancing, in a private courtyard of Jerusalem some found a creative way of keeping the quorum of ten men required for the public prayer by counting the men on their balcony. A Cohen, would perform the ritual priestly blessing from his balcony, like the pope during his *urbi et orbi* address.[2]

---

[2] A *Cohen* is a descendant of Aaron, the first Hebrew High Priest.

Later in New York, when Dani was recounting the story using the French for priestly blessing (*bénédiction sacerdotale*), the word *bénédiction* was mistakenly understood to mean baptism by Dani's friend, who then associated *sacerdotale* with the Christian religion. They understood what Dani was saying only when Dani used the Hebrew expression (*birkat cohanim*), instead of its French translation.

Dani felt she was walking like a blind woman, as if just waking up and not being sure yet of the reality. Words were telescoping into each other, and she felt that she was talking a language of one, used only by her, and not even understood clearly by her, since she knew her word associations were not fully conscious.[3] Fluidity of language. Even the same word

---

[3] When Dani would reach the early blessing portion of the morning prayers, she would find a gendered choice. It was the only place in the entire traditional Hebrew prayer book where men and women had different blessings. The men were expected to say the blessing for God "who did not make me a woman," while the women were expected to use the blessing for God "who made me according to His will."

Dani always felt that the women's blessing was more beautiful than the men's blessing. Acceptance of who one is, acceptance of her identity and limitations was an important value which transcended gender and physical differences. She had enjoyed working on being grateful for what she made of herself, and she was comfortable with her blessing. The man's blessing appeared disparaging of women. And Dani did not understand that. She asked the Rebetzin, the wife of her Rabbi, if she was uncomfortable with the men's blessing. Not at all, the Rebetzin answered. They do not have to experience the pain of childbirth. Dani could accept that answer with a smile from this pious woman who had many children herself. Dani had never given birth, and who was she to judge the Rebetzin and her faith. The Rebetzin was right, it was a good way of seeming to excuse the male chauvinist wording of the men's blessing while subverting it into a recognition of women's suffering.

The whispered blessing muffled the almost imperceptible rustle as she adjusted her off-centered skirt. Dani tried to concentrate on her

with a different intonation had different meanings and layers. *Daniel*, for example. In English the first syllable was accentuated: **DA**niel. In Hebrew the second syllable was accentuated: Da**NI**el; and in French it was the third: Dan**IEL**. In French, the masculine[ii] first name Daniel was pronounced the same way as its feminine counterpart: Danielle. However in English, the French pronunciation of the male name Daniel was reserved for the female name Danielle. In Hebrew Da**NI**el was unequivocally male, while in English, Dan**IEL** was unequivocally female. Dani felt he was walking like a blind man, as if just waking up and not being sure yet of the reality. Words were telescoping into each other, and he felt that he was talking a language of one, understood only by him.[4]

---

[3](cont.) prayers. She ignored the gendered expression of God, and did not pay attention to the absence of references to the founding mothers. She tried to focus on the written Hebrew words of the payer book. Blessed be You, God, our God... However her mind wandered through the lattice down the balcony, as she was finishing her blessing. If she saw him, she would invite him to come and talk with her during the afternoon. His sure presence was comforting. She could sense that he liked her more than a friend, but she was not attracted to him. In a moment of unhappiness, he had asked her out

[once. She had]

[4] When Dani would reach the early blessing portion of the morning prayers, he was not comfortable saying the man's part, and blessing God for not having made him a woman. He knew the interpretation that his Rabbi had given him. One thanks God for giving us commandments, and men had more commandments to observe than women. This was the reason of thanking God for not making him a woman. Nevertheless, Dani had blessing envy and, instead of his assigned blessing, he choose to recite the women's blessing which he found more meaningful and which could also be applied to all human beings, including men. Dani smiled at his secret little rebellion; but he

once. She had rebuffed him gently. And they never talked about it afterward, acting as if it had never happened. When she needed companionship, or had issues with her lover or, after a while, if she wanted to inquire about his current wellbeing, she would call him and he would be there. The blessing. Blessed be You, God, our God… She had to finish her blessing. She had confided to him things only good friends would. She was not sure that he had done the same with her. THE BLESSING. They never touched. And especially now, everyone was *shomer negiah*,[5] even the non-religious guys. He would correct her English sometimes. Blessed be You, God, our God, King of the world, who made me according to His wishes. The grammar may have worked in Hebrew, but it was disjointed in English. He would not have written it this way. He looked at the lattice separating men and women in the synagogue. Did he notice her? She was not sure. Maybe he was looking at other women? She could not tell. The blessing. Was she looking at him? He knew it was hopeless. He accepted the crumbs of her presence. Her attention was comforting and he genuinely cared about her. He was not jealous of her friend, who was younger and clearly attractive. But he would not mess with her. That was sacred. Once a former girlfriend of a very good friend made advances to him. Although she and his friend had been separated for a long time, he knew how much his friend used to like her (they had used his room once) and he felt that it would be betraying him. THE BLESSING. Younger and clearly attractive. Now was not the time. High heels, nice warm smile. He knew too much about her. Sacred. It was sacred. There are things you don't mess with. THE BLESSING. Blessed be You, God, our God, King of the world, who did not make me a

---

could not in good conscience utter the original blessing assigned to him.

[5] Literally means "observant of touch" in Hebrew. The term refers to someone who follows the Jewish tradition of refraining from physical contact with members of the opposite sex.

woman. No. Not this one. The other blessing. He had heard a muffled rustle, or thought he had, when he noticed her adjusting her skirt. **THE BLESSING.** Blessed be You, God, our God, Ruler of the words, who made me according to Your wishes. God, the Ruler of the words, the Word Ruler.

New York, May 10, 2020

NOTES

[i] (page 23): In French "souvenir" can mean, as in English, an object reminding us of a place we visited. However, unlike in English, "souvenir" in French can also be a synonym for a memory ("memoire" in French).

[ii] (page 25): "Masculine" in English is the equivalent of the adjective *"masculin"* in French. The word "masculine" exists in French; oddly, it is the feminine form of "masculine." For example, "la circoncision masculine" (male circumcision) or "une femme masculine" (a masculine woman). It is normal to say in English the first name *Daniel* is a man's name. However, it would sound strange to say in French *"Daniel* est masculine."

In Hebrew too, *'Arel* is a word that contains an inherent contradiction. *'Arel* (ערל) means uncircumcised. By extension it means a non-Jew. *'Arelit* (ערלית), the feminine form in ancient Hebrew (more commonly used currently in Yiddish, and pronounced *arelis*), means a non-Jewish woman. Literally it means an "uncircumcised woman," implying that Jewish women are circumcised. However, in Judaism, there is no female "circumcision." Circumcision, according to the Torah, symbolizes the covenant (*brit* in Hebrew) between God and Abraham and between God and the Jewish people. Although they are not physically circumcised, Jewish women are fully a part of this covenant with God. In Hebrew, the association between the word "covenant," *brit* (pronounced *bris* in Yiddish), and the word

27

"circumcision" (*brit milah* in Hebrew, or just *bris* in Yiddish) is so strong that *bris* is now a commonly used euphemism for penis in Yiddish.

This male/female (con)fusing polarity may also be applied to God. After times of suffering and maledictions, God is said to remember His(/Her?) covenant with the Jewish people, and with the descendants of its founding fathers, the biblical figures Abraham, Isaac and Jacob. God remembers?

Does God forget? Dani listened to the Rabbi in front of the Holy Ark commenting on the *parasha*, the weekly Torah portion. **In our *parasha*, God warns the Hebrews that a long series of awful maledictions follows disobedience to the Torah. However, later in our *parasha*, we are assured that God will "remember" the covenant made with Abraham, Isaac and Jacob (and by extension with the entire Jewish people) (Lev. 26:42). As a result, blessings will end the curses. God is supposed to be all-knowing, so *forgetting* for God means: turning His face away, not paying attention. God, according traditional rabbinic teaching, has different attributes, for example an attribute of Judgement (*Din*, in Hebrew), and an attribute of Lovingkindness (*Hesed*, in Hebrew). When God remembers the suffering of his creatures, God emphasizes the Divine attribute of Lovingkindness; and when God turns away from them, the emphasis is on Judgement.**

The Kabbalah expands and personalizes this traditional view of the attributes into different *emanations* of the Divine that are called *sefirot*. Lovingkindness is associated with Abraham and is viewed as a masculine aspect of God. Judgement (corresponding to the emanation called *Gevura* or Strength) is associated with the feminine aspect of the Divine. So what does it mean when in our *parasha* God

28

mentions remembering God's covenant (*brit*)? Let's look at the text of Leviticus 26:42:

> Then I will remember My covenant "Jacob," and also My covenant "Isaac," and I will remember also My covenant "Abraham."

According to an allegorical interpretation in the Midrash Aggadah, the seemingly superfluous Hebrew word "*et*" before "*brit*" (covenant) was written to include the covenant with the founding mothers. It is a traditional approach to interpret additional or missing words in the biblical text.

If we want also to understand the simple apparent meaning of the text, we need to add the missing "with" before the names of the fathers Abraham, Isaac and Jacob. Without adding "with" we would read that Abraham is literally one of the names of God's covenant. Paradoxically, we could still read this biblical text very literally through the lens of the Kabbalah, the esoteric interpretation:

> I, God, expressing now My feminine attribute of Judgment, will ultimately awaken My previously dormant masculine attribute of Lovingkindness, My *brit* which is called "Abraham," My masculine expression.

The circumcision of Abraham, the father of the faithful, is paralleled in the previous verse with the circumcision of the heart which was lacking to the unfaithful people. Leviticus 26:41 talks about the uncircumcised heart of the Hebrews as being responsible for God's wrath and for the curses.

Why is the verb "remember" in Hebrew (*zakhar* זכר) and in Aramaic (*dekhar* דכר) the same as the noun for male? A literal explanation would point out that in a patriarchal society remembering meant tracing back through the male lineage. However, if we pursue our esoteric explanation, the verb *ezkor* (אזכר), which in Hebrew means, literally "I will remember," could be translated instead as "I will render male," which would fit nicely with our last translation: "I will awaken My previously dormant male attribute." The equivalent Arabic verb (*dakkara* ذَكَّر) literally means both "to remind" and "to make [a word] masculine". In Hebrew, outside a usage most likely borrowed from the Arabic grammarians, we can only esoterically allude to this double meaning of the verb *ezkor*.

Both attributes are needed, male and female, Lovingkindness and Judgment. Those of us who are parents or educators know that love is necessary but not enough when raising a child. It is also essential to set limits. Only when God is united harmoniously within both aspects of the Divine, male and female, only then can blessings overcome the curses.

The Rabbi's speech made an impression on Dani. At a previous sermon, Dani recalled that the Rabbi had mentioned that God's prayer mirrors the prayers made by the people of Israel. Israel praises the unity of God in the Jewish profession of faith, the *Shema*. God's prayer praises the uniqueness of the people of Israel. Could this parallel be used also for the rest of the prayers? Would God choose to praise an Israel who did not render Him as female? Wouldn't God prefer to praise Israel who rendered God according to their will? This comforted Dani in his choice of blessings earlier this morning.

Dani was uncomfortable with the notion of females seen as strict enforcers of justice, and men as forgiving and loving. Not because this runs counter to Western stereotypes, but because women were associated with curses and men with blessings. Nevertheless, Dani understood the Rabbi's message that God included at the same time masculine and feminine aspects, and that both were needed. Did that mean that since humans were created in God's image, she also had to harmonize her own masculine and feminine attributes? Did that mean that her lover also had masculine attributes? Would she, like God, be accepting her attributes for herself? Blessed be You, God, our God, Ruler of the world, who made me in Your image.

The rabbi continued: **In Genesis (1:27), God created the first human, Adam, in God's image, both male and female. Later on, God separated both sides (*tsela'*) into male and female (Gen 2:21). This is how the rabbis have understood the Hebrew word *tsela'* (צלע) in that verse, not as "rib" (*côte* in French) but as "side" (*côté* in French). According to the Zohar, each face of the original Adam, male and female, was composed of both aspects, Lovingkindness and Judgment. Even the male aspect of Adam had a female component, Judgment; and even the female aspect of Adam had a male component, Lovingkindness (Zohar III, 117a). After the separation of the androgynous first human into male and female, human souls continue to emerge as male and female together. When they descend, they become separated as male and female, only to hopefully be reunited by God in this world (Zohar I, 85b).[1] In his book *Maor VaShamesh*, the Hasidic Rabbi, Rabbi Kalonymos Kalman Epstein (1751-1823), relates a vision he had of messianic times when everyone will perfect their soul back to its root, and when there will no longer be categories of masculine and feminine, for all will come to realize equally God's divine light. The *Maor***

31

VaShamesh views Miriam the prophetess as having been closer than Moses to that highest apprehension. When they both sang after the crossing of the Red Sea, Moses uses the future "I will sing to God" (Exod 15:1) because he spoke while still under the categories of masculine and feminine, before the light of supernal clarity had been manifested. But Miriam drew down the eternal light and she tells the women "sing now to God." By making a circle-dance, she drew down the supernal light from the source where the categories of masculine and feminine do not exist.[2]

May we all merit having our souls reach Miriam's level and draw from the eternal light. Shabbat shalom.

Amen, responded Dani.

New York, 21st of Iyyar, 5780
Eve of Shabbat Behar-Bechukotai
36th day of the Omer

---

[1] (page 31): Isaiah Tishby, *The wisdom of the Zohar*, translated by David Goldstein. The Littman Library of Jewish Civilization, 1989, page 1381
[2] (page 32): Norman Lamm, *The religious thoughts of Hasidism*, The Michael Scharf Publication Trust of Yeshiva University Press, 1999, page 602.

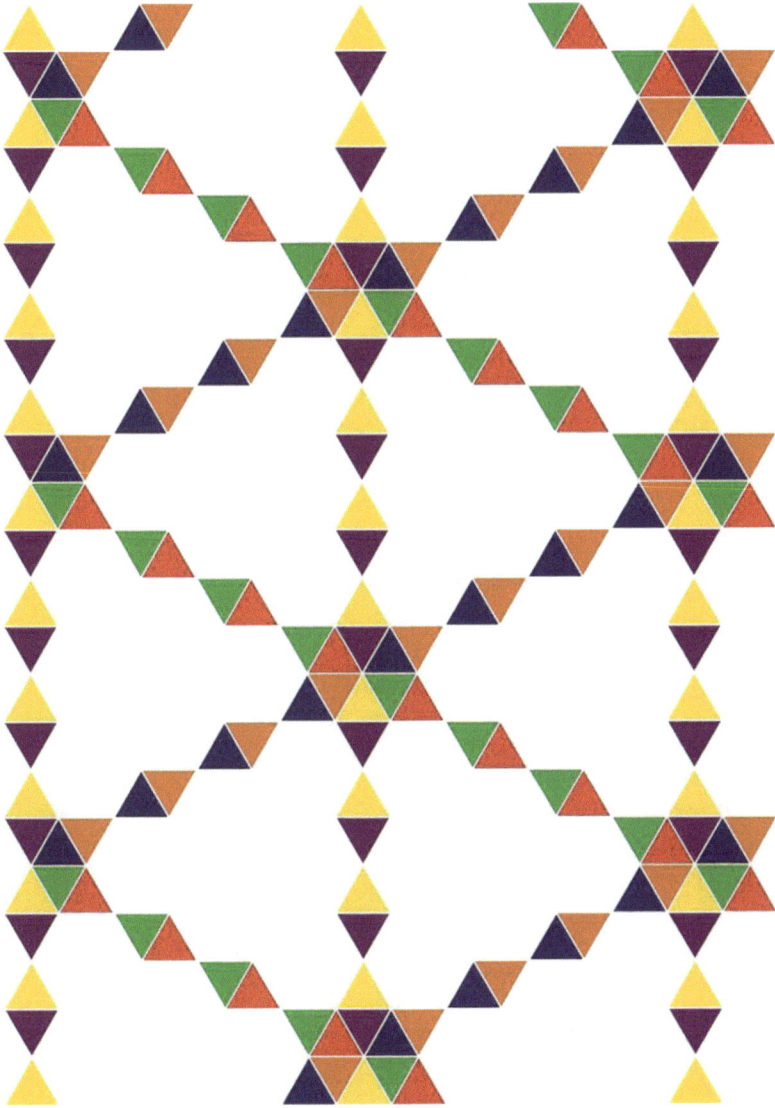

33

4 Gourmandize

Gourmandise

(Gourmandize)

Ça va. Le boulot va bien. Un peu ennuyeux côté maison. Alors quand j'ai du temps je lis, et j'écris (en anglais uniquement ces temps-ci). Quelques rencontres virtuelles. Une parisienne confinée, une chanteuse dans le Nord des USA qui a le mal du pays et le mal de la mer. La mer lui manque. Mais la mer lui est interdite. Ne pas laisser les orteils s'enfoncer dans le sable où la mer pulse et le vent iodé laisse un goût salé. Goûte-moi! Goûte-moi, m'a demandé une Québécoise. Alors je l'ai goûtée. La mer. Un jour nous nous y replongerons. C'est pour bientôt. Ici on commence à se déconfiner. Les fleuristes sont créatifs. Les fleurs c'est essentiel? Pour l'amour bien sûr, pour la mort pas sûr. Alors on rajoute quelques frissons à l'étalage, les fruits sont essentiels, non? Alors on ouvre le magasin et on peut vendre ses fleurs. Allez mes belles livrez des oranges et des pommes à votre amour, rajoutez quelques chastes baisers sur les marguerites, il m'aime un peu beaucoup à la folie même un peu c'est déjà bien, laissez-vous goûter mes fruits mûrs à point, mûres noires avec quelques points encore rouges coccinelle inversée. Alors oui moi ça va. Et toi, ils te laissent tranquille au boulot ?

New York,
Le 20 mai, 2020

36

Gourmandize

I'm fine. The job is going well. A little boring on the home front. So when I have time, I read and I write (in English only these days). Some virtual encounters. A confined Parisian woman, a singer in the North of the USA who is homesick and seasick (she misses the sea). But the sea is forbidden to her. Don't let your toes sink in the sand where the sea throbs and the wind leaves a salty taste. Taste me! *Taste me*, a Quebec woman asked me. So I tasted it. The sea. One day we will plunge back into it. It will happen soon. Here we begin to de-confine ourselves. The florists are creative. Flowers are essential? For love, of course. For death, not sure. So we add a few frissons to the display. *Les fruits sont essentiels, non?* Fruits are essential, right? Then you open the store, and you can sell your flowers. Come on my beautiful ones, deliver oranges and apples to your love, add some chaste kisses on the daisies, he loves me a little bit, madly. Even a little bit is already good, let yourself taste my ripe fruits, blackberries with a few red dots— inverted ladybug. So yes, I'm fine. And you, do they leave you alone at work?

New York
May 20, 2020
Translated from the original in French

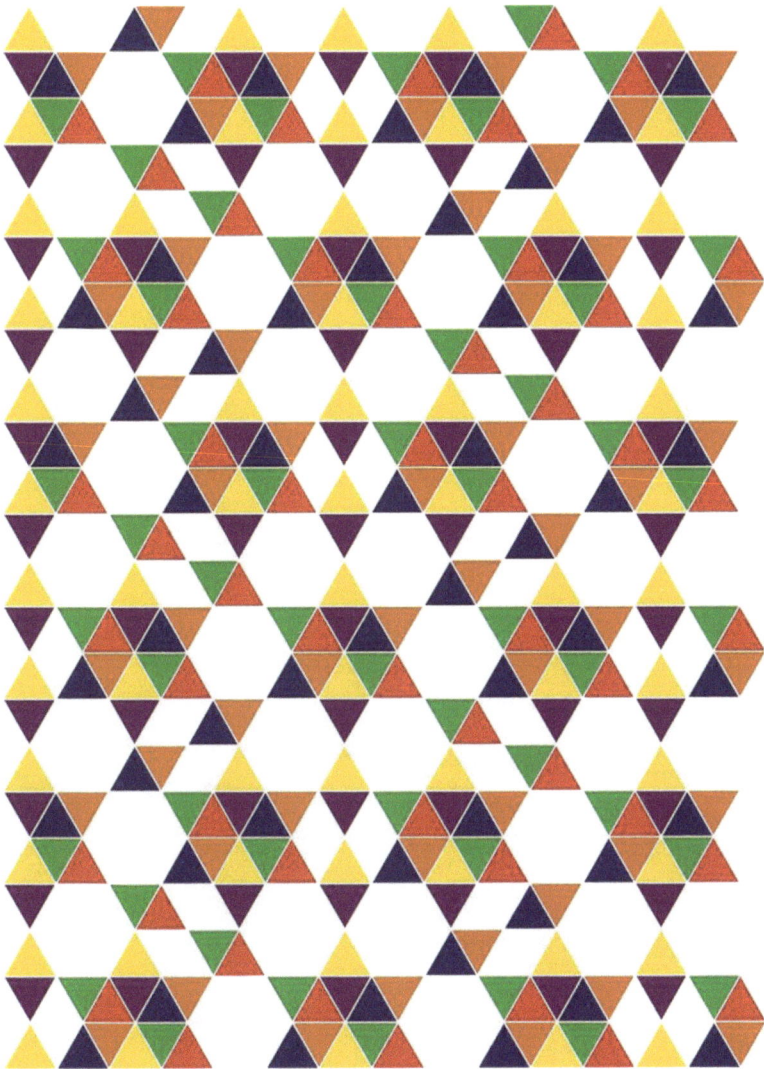

5 Concealed

Concealed

Pensive, lying in a pose of complete abandon, with an inward-turning gaze… Vulnerable, open, rosy cheeks on milk white skin, resting after the storm, unveiled, impassive, unconcerned by Xiaoping's look or by a clothed black woman smoking next to her, with closed long legs on the couch, a relaxed, bent hand touching her own lips, more arched than Adam's hand in Leonardo's creation of man, with both eyes shining through a face half concealed by darkness, the only concealed portion of this motionless tableau.[1] Enigmatic. Indecipherable. Inaccessible.

They never could talk. Xiaoping didn't even know the name of this remote creature, however close, so close, within hand's reach. What happened? This rosacea was not an illness of the skin, but maybe of the heart, *la maladie d'amour*, the disease of love. The naked truth was hidden by a cloak of invisibility. Available to all, but covered in mystery. Who was the black woman? An attendant? Too independent. A lover? Too uninvolved. A matron in charge of keeping the young chaste? A boss protecting a defenseless worker? Xiaoping was lost in contemplation of the pure creamy body. A subtle palette of whites was needed to render the silkiness of the skin, the bright point of light in the center of the pupils, even the pupil of the right eye blurred in the shadow. As long as Xiaoping officiated, with his brushes dipping delicately in the colors freshly squeezed from their tubes, he could look the model in the eyes, as a young hospital intern distances himself, or tries to, in his white doctor's coat from an enticing beauty or a powerful ephebe. Xiaoping could not look at the Holy of Holies covered loosely with her hand, or he might get lost.[2] Xiaoping had a friend, a model, who once told him that you get used to posing naked and having all eyes on you, looking at you. But dressing and undressing is another story; it is done alone. You do not want people's eyes on you while you dress or undress. For this, you retreat to the dressing area, enclosed by curtains, where you are hidden. Even after they saw you posing nude for hours, you still need your privacy. While getting dressed you would want to be hidden.[3]

Xiaoping thought he knew her from another life. Had she ever looked at him? Had they been together? Had they been betrothed? Did he covet her? Had he ever pronounced her the vow of love?

I will betroth you to me forever
I will betroth you to me
In righteousness and in justice
In lovingkindness and in mercy
I will betroth you to me in faithfulness[4]

Will he ever?

New York
May 24, 2002

Sources

[1] Was Xiaoping looking at a live model? Was he looking at a man or a woman? Was it a painting he was contemplating? Maybe Félix Vallotton's take on Manet's Olympia?

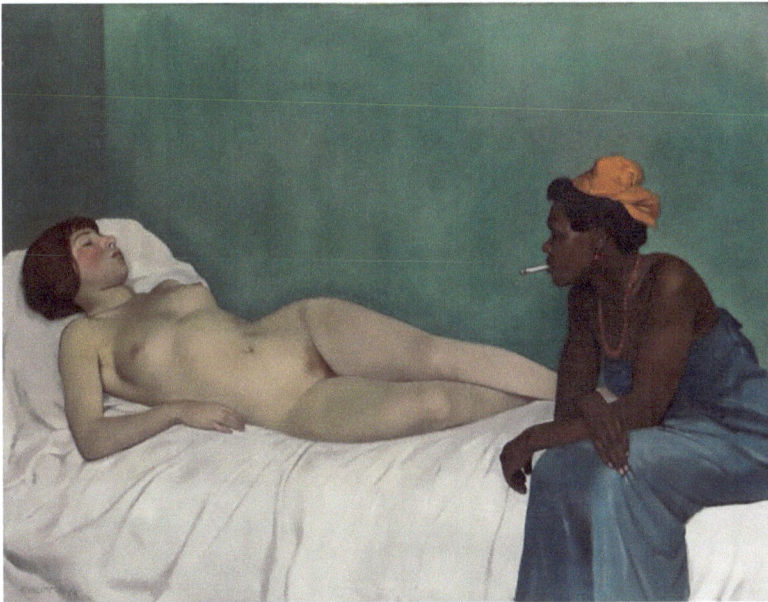

Félix Vallotton, *The White and the Black (La Blanche et la Noire)*, 1913. Photograph: © Kunstmuseum Bern; Hahnloser/Jaeggli Foundation, Villa Flora, Winterthur.

Only in Vallotton's painting is the black woman smoking, and only in Manet's painting is the model covering herself with her hand.

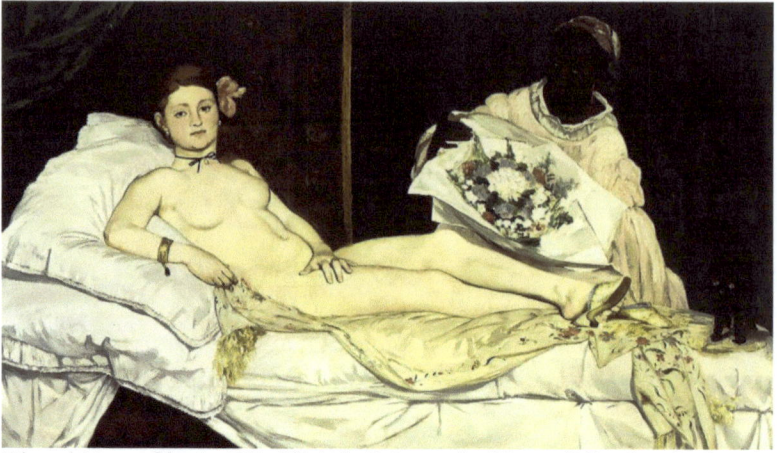

Edouard Manet: *Olympia*, 1863 (RF 644); Paris, musée d'Orsay. (Offered to the State by public subscription on the initiative of Claude Monet. Reprinted with permission.)

Neither painting has the model's face partly in the shadow. In Vallotton's painting, the model's eyes are closed. Maybe Xiaoping was thinking of the Chinese photographer, Yang Fudong.

沉思的 *Chénsī de (Pensive)*, 1993

In that black and white photograph, the model's right eye is in shadow and the hand more flexed than in Michelangelo's painting of Adam's creation.

46

Michelangelo, *The Creation of Adam*, 1510 (fresco) (detail from the Sistine Chapel ceiling)

However in the photo, the model appears fully clothed, while in the story *Concealed*, the model cannot be fully clothed.

[2] **"Do this for them, that they may live and not die when they approach the Holy of Holies: let the officiant and his sons assign them, each man according to his worship and his charge. They should not come looking when the Holy is being covered, or they will die."** (Num 4:19-20, translation by the author).

Some commentators explain that the interdiction is against having a glimpse of the divine presence before the Holy objects are fully covered. However if we follow the text literally, and sometimes a literal interpretation can actually be a more metaphorical one, the text only talks about the danger of looking at the Holy being concealed.

[3] The act of covering and uncovering is more intimate than the state of just being uncovered. A dress which stops well below the knee would be considered modest. However, if we add fabric and lengthen the dress with a slit in it, even if the top of the slit stops well under the knee, this extra covering below the appropriate length is more revealing than the absence of concealment:

47

"**A slit in a skirt attracts attention to the legs because as the wearer walks her legs continuously appear and disappear. In some strides, more shows, while in others, less shows. (...) Just as an advertisement that continuously lights up, switches off and lights up again catches people's attention, so legs that continuously appear and disappear are highly conspicuous. (...) A slit in a garment is forbidden because of *pritzus* [breach of modesty]. It is forbidden even if thick tights are being worn. It is forbidden even if the complete slit is below the knee.**" (Pesach Eliyahu Falk, *Oz VeHadar Levusha. Modesty: An Adornment for Life*, Feldheim Publishers, 1998, pp 319-320)

The concealment by a hand, or the darkness around an eye is enticing us to uncover more. Similarly, and mirroring the physical body, Menahem Mendel Schneerson (as understood by Wolfson) wrote about yearning of redemption within darkness:

"**Just as the darkness is greatest right before dawn, the need to propagate secrets is proportionate to the intensification of their concealment. Paradoxically, then, the dark itself is proof of the imminence of redemption, and the more one thinks about the darkness, the more one will think about the light.**" Elliot R. Wolfson, *Open secret: Postmessianic Messianism and the Mystical Revision of Menahem Mendel Schneerson*. Columbia University Press, New York, 2009, page 36)

[4] Hosea 2:21-22

New York
1st of Sivan, 5780

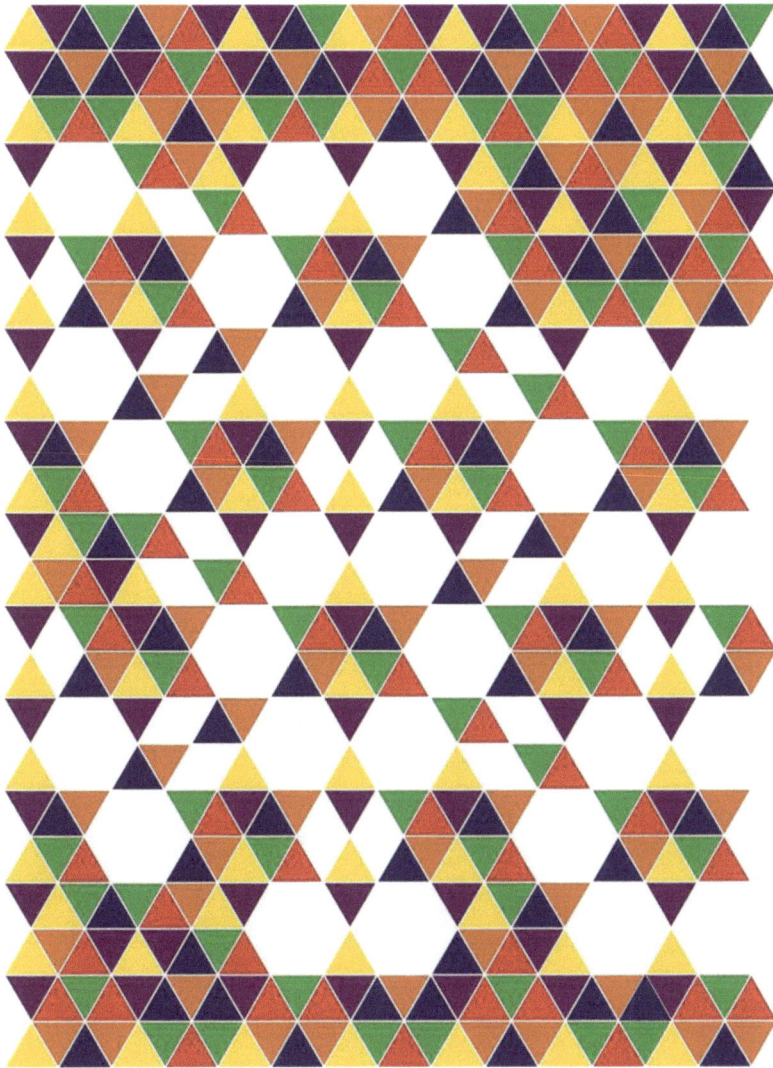

49

6 Colorful Words

The small hand-size tape recorder was hidden by the night table, while Messaoud entered the bedroom where his daughter, along with her husband and son, waited for him. A far-away father and grandfather, but a father nevertheless. Why was it hidden? Why not be open about taping him? Maybe he would have refused? Maybe he would have agreed, but knowing he was being recorded would have made him self-conscious? Did she want to have a voice equivalent of a candid picture of her father? But then why, when he left, didn't she tell him about the tape? Why did she leave the tape deposited with her son? Why was the tape lost?

Yes, the tape had been lost. For years, François, Messaoud's grandson, had looked for it. An unmarked tape which he had probably recorded over, like what happened later with the tape marked "Rien" ("nothing" in French). He had made a compilation of his favorite music, a few minutes each of the different styles, from Nina Hagen to Russian folk songs, and he had given it to a woman friend. She had loved it but couldn't find it when she looked for it again. She must have recorded over that tape labeled "Rien." Or, like that recording he had made by mistake, taping a phone conversation with another girl, not really flirting, just talking, but the dialogue was all in the blanks, between the words, with their never-disclosed mutual interest. Toward the end of the call, he realized that he had been recording the entire conversation and he had asked her if he could keep the tape and use it, maybe to get inspired for a play. She had said yes. And now, all that was left were the blanks and the holes. The words must have been recorded over, and the play was never written, and she never became his girlfriend. All that is left is the story. The story of a missed story. A misstory. A mystery.

And you should know by now what the tape captured by chance when Messaoud entered his grandson's bedroom. A grandson he hardly knew. A grandson whose dearest memory of him was when they were in a car and he was sitting on Messaoud's lap and pretending to sleep for what seemed a long time. François felt warmth when Messaoud held his head gently, protecting him from the movement of the car and enveloping his pretend sleep with care and maybe love.

And love it was (or was it?) when, as soon as he entered the room, he placed the palms of his hands on his grandson's head and recited the ancient words. The only voice recording François once had of his grandfather was the priestly blessing.

May God bless you and guard you.

The words were stitched with love, each letter shining its own bright moving color, spelling the calm majestic, compassionate, comforting and peaceful ancestral blessings with blue, purple, red, pink or orange, covering the child's head warmly, connecting generations, families and communities.

May God shine His face toward you and give you grace.

Each thread was sewn by caring hands, from family and friends invited to participate in the confection of the blessings, to add a letter around each corner, to wrap the body of the child within a communal quilt of tenderness.

May God raise His face toward you and place you in peace.
(Num 6:24-26)

And the mother, who dispensed the priestly blessing to her daughters, received herself the same gift of love from her friends and family, an embroidered prayer shawl with the same colorful words of peace and serenity.

And the son too, the son who was the recipient of the ephemeral grandfatherly blessing, contributed a red letter for the mother of the daughters, although the words of blessing had been ephemeral, too, between them and although their peace was socially distant, respectful, without love but peace nevertheless. And that too was still a precious blessing. A blessing from a time when we could still be close to each other and when we could pass a needle or a thread or a corner of a prayer shawl, from hand to hand, from heart to heart.

A remote and passing time, a blessed time.

New York
May 28, 2020

Letters of the Priestly Blessing stitched on the corner of a prayer shawl. Artwork by Daniel Rosen.

7 Coping with Anticipated Trauma through Culturally-Informed Fictional Narrative: From the Holocaust to the COVID-19 Pandemic.

Abstract

Anticipating traumatic experiences can induce intense distress and fear. Construction of fictional narratives can help with coping with that fear by externalizing it. Because it is fictional, it permits us to think and talk safely about the unspeakable. Creative writing can explore meanings for an imagined exposure to an anticipated trauma, and can help prepare for it, and integrate previous chaotic and fragmented traumatic experiences. These stories can foster connections by providing their narrators and readers with a testimony that can be witnessed and shared. As an illustration, we describe and analyze such a constructed fictional narrative. Being grounded in cultural and religious references or symbols connects the narrator with a community and its collective narrative. This culturally-specific approach could be adapted across different settings and cultures, from trauma of the Holocaust in the past, into current traumatic situations, such as those related to the COVID-19 pandemic.

Introduction

The world has experienced an understandable fear related to the COVID-19 pandemic which, at the time of this writing, continues to ebb and flow. Writing fictional trauma narrative can help master the fear of such an anticipated trauma.

Narrative and trauma

Gwozdziewycz and Mehl-Madrona (2013) found, in their meta-analysis, that narrative therapy was effective in addressing trauma or posttraumatic stress disorder in refugees.

Pennebaker advocates using creative writing (what he calls *expressive writing*) therapeutically not only with past trauma, but also about imagined traumatic events. In one exercise, he suggests choosing a traumatic experience that "ideally …is the least relevant to your life" (Pennebaker, 2004, p. 141).

Furer et al. (2007) proposed that writing about exposure to an anticipated trauma could be a valuable coping strategy for the fear of the future.

We will review different characteristics of such a narrative: Exposure, externalization, meaning, and connection with others.

Exposure

Menzies et al. (2018) reported a variety of cognitive and behavioral procedures proposed as means to reduce death anxiety: exposure therapy, behavioral experiments, cognitive reappraisal, and existential psychotherapy.

In their literature review, Robjant and Fazel (2010) found that Narrative Exposure Therapy (NET), a short-term therapy for individuals who have PTSD symptoms, was efficacious in reducing PTSD among children.

Externalization

White and Epston (1990) proposed externalizing a problem (e.g., an intense fear) as part of their narrative therapy technique. The problem is viewed as being outside the person and can be addressed as if it were a separate entity.

The written recollection of a past trauma can enable the narrator to externalize the trauma and master a chaotic and frightening past by turning it into an organized and meaningful story. According to Richman (2013, p. 13):

> The ability to step outside of oneself and see the product that one has created through the eyes of another (i.e., the witness) allows a person to shift perspective and achieve some distance—a state that is helpful to gain mastery over the chaotic feelings that follow in the wake of trauma.

Likewise, I suggest that a fictional narrative about an anticipated trauma can help process fear by creating a distance from the trauma through externalization.

Meaning

Creative writing can be used to explore the meanings of overwhelming and fragmenting traumatic experiences, past and current, merging with an anticipated trauma. Victor Frankl (1985, p. 95) found meaning by externalizing his traumatic experience, as if he was already outside the camp:

"I was giving a lecture on the psychology of the concentration camp!"

Tomer and Eliason (1996) suggest that an integrative, comprehensive model of death anxiety needs to include and explore past-related regret, future-related regret, and the 'meaningfulness' of death: "Meaningfulness of death refers to one's concept of death and ability to make sense of it."

Connection with others

While creating their narrative in solitude, authors can connect mentally and emotionally with their families and friends. The completed text of the story allows its author to also connect more broadly by having others witness the described experience and provide feedback, support, and recognition (Bolton, 2008). The connection with others is crucial in attempting to heal from trauma, which can be isolating. Frankl (in the above quote) sees himself not as alone, but as a member of a community of scientists. This connection helped him maintain a meaningful identity as a psychiatry professor within that community.

Culturally-informed narrative

The inclusion in the story of relevant cultural or religious references or symbols helps narrators connect with their particular community and relate with its collective narrative. Witztum and Goodman (1999) suggest using a culturally-adapted narrative paradigm for the understanding and treatment of mental disorders.

According to Terror Management Theory, cultural worldviews manage the terror associated with the awareness of death by imbuing the universe with order and meaning, and by promising protection and death transcendence. (Greenberg, Solomon, and Pyszczynski, 1997).

Furer et al. (2007) encourage imaginal exposure to symptoms of feared illnesses that are difficult to reproduce in real life (p. 113). They propose that the exposure "be conducted in a graduated fashion with the illness stories becoming more anxiety-provoking and having more difficult endings (e.g., painful death) as the client progresses through the exposure" (p. 119). In their handout, given to patients about creating an illness story, they tell patients to write the story in the first person "to make the story more real for you." They report that "our experience has been that introducing these strategies early in treatment can result in substantial reductions of avoidance and anxiety" (p. 128).

We argue that although an illness narrative in the first person may be a more vivid form of exposure, using the third person with a fictional character may be the only acceptable option in certain cultures. For example, there is a popular Jewish superstition to avoid saying something which could be seen as tempting fate.[6] Therefore, it might be difficult for traditional Jews to describe their own deaths in the first person. Rather, such a story would probably not elicit social support, and would likely be met with reprobation, along with a response to ward off the Evil Eye; it would tend to cause undue anxiety. The power of words is so great that they can have a healing effect and even replace sacred rituals which are

---

[6] The injunction, "Don't open your mouth to the devil" (in Hebrew: *Al Tiftach Peh Lasatan*) is still in use today. It is mentioned in the Talmud (Ketuvot 8b, Brachot 19a) and refers to the idea of not inviting misfortune. This concern is seen across many cultures. Risen and Gilovich (2018) report that "one of the most pervasive and powerful superstitions is the belief that it is bad luck to "tempt fate."

now impossible to perform.[7] In the narrative example we are presenting, we will discuss how the story itself could be viewed as an attempt to replace a religious ritual. Rituals have been used for the treatment of trauma (Johnson et al., 1995).

Under the cover of fiction, the narrative may permit an avenue to more safely speak about the unspeakable. Likewise, in mysticism, concealment has been described as a necessary step for the ability to reveal. [8]

Summary

We advocate for the construction of a narrative grounded in the cultural and religious background of the narrator. Especially when it is culturally relevant, as in the narrative we are presenting, we encourage the construction of an illness story which not only describes fictional events, but also utilizes a fictional character.

The construction of this fictional narrative can be a therapeutic tool in helping individuals distressed by the anticipation of a significant trauma. The repeated imagining of exposure to an anticipated trauma, for example by re-writing or re-reading the narrative, could attenuate the anxiety response to the trauma. The narrative can explore how past experience of trauma exacerbates the impact of future trauma.

---

[7] For example: "Rabbi Yehoshua ben Levi says: 'The prayers were instituted to replace the daily sacrifices...' [in the destroyed Jerusalem Temple]" (Talmud Brachot 26b); Telling a Hasidic story replaces a lost ritual (Scholem, 1954, p. 350). Rituals have been shown to have a healing power during psychotherapy with Orthodox Jewish patients (Greenberg and Witztum, 2001, p. 270-289).
[8] God reveals Himself by concealing His infinite light, garbed in the letters and words of the Torah (Wolfson, 2009, p. 32 and 159).

Outside of a formal therapy setting, this fictional narrative could be used as a self-therapy tool to provide insight for writers or therapists.

One limitation to the use of fictional narrative in therapy is that it may not be ideal for individuals who are not particularly adept at creative writing or at using metaphors.

To illustrate the potential benefit of composing an imaginary trauma narrative, we present a fictional narrative by a fictional woman named Malka. Along with this narrative entitled "ONE," we present a commentary which explains its specific cultural references and highlights the underlying coping mechanisms in its construction.

BIBLIOGRAPHY

Bolton, G. (2008). "Writing is a way of saying things I can't say"-therapeutic creative writing: a qualitative study of its value to people with cancer cared for in cancer and palliative healthcare. *Medical Humanities*. Vol.34(1), 40-46.

Frankl, V. E. (1985 [originally 1946]). *Man's Search for Meaning*. New York: Washington Square Press.

Furer, P., Walker, J. R. and Stein, M. B. (2007), *Treating Health Anxiety and Fear of Death A Practitioner's Guide*. New York, NY : Springer New York : Imprint: Springer 2007.

Greenberg, J., Solomon, S. and Pyszczynski, T. (1997). *Terror management theory of self-esteem and cultural worldviews: Empirical assessments and conceptual refinements*. In P. M. Zanna (Ed.), Advances in experimental social psychology (Vol. 29, pp. 61–139). San Diego, CA: Academic Press, Inc..

Greenberg, D. and Witztum, E. (2001). *Sanity and sanctity: Mental health work among the Ultra-Orthodox in Jerusalem*. New Haven, CT: Yale University Press.

Gwozdziewycz, N. and Mehl-Madrona, L. (2013) *Meta-analysis of the use of narrative exposure therapy for the effects of trauma among refugee* *populations.* The Permanente journal, 2013, Vol.17(1), pp.70-6

Menzies, R. E., Zuccala, M., Sharpe, L. and Dar-Nimrod, I. (2018) The effects of psychosocial interventions on death anxiety: A meta-analysis and systematic review of randomised controlled trials. *Journal of Anxiety Disorders,* October 2018, Vol.59, pp.64-73

Pennebaker, J. W. (2004). *Writing to Heal: A guided journal for recovering from trauma and emotional upheaval.* Wheat Ridge, CO: Center for Journal Therapy, Inc.

Richman, S. (2014). *Mended by the Muse: Creative Transformations of Trauma.* Routeledge: New York and London.

Risen, J. L. and Gilovich, T. (2018). Understanding people's fear of tempting fate. *Journal of the Association for Consumer Research,* 3, 599-611.

Robjant, K. and Fazel, M. (2010). The emerging evidence for Narrative Exposure Therapy: A review. *Clinical Psychology Review,* 30(8), 1030-1039. doi:10.1016/j.cpr.2010.07.004

Scholem G. G. (1954 [originally 1941]). *Major Trends in Jewish Mysticism.* Schocken Books, New York.

Tomer A. and Eliason G. (1996). Toward a comprehensive model of death anxiety. *Death Studies,* 20, 343-365.

White, M., and Epston, D. (1990). *Narrative means to a therapeutic ends.* New York: Norton.

Witztum, E. and Goodman, Y. (1999). Narrative Construction of Distress and Therapy: A Model Based on Work with Ultra-Orthodox Jews. *Transcultural Psychiatry,* 12/1999, Vol.36(4), 403-436

Wolfson, E. R. (2009) *Open Secret: Postmessianic Messianism and the Mystical Revision of Menahem Mendel Schneerson.* New York: Columbia University Press.

8 "ONE"

New York
June 14, 2010

"ONE"
The Story of Malka Risze

It was too late for the lights. For Yiddish, press "ONE." For English, press "TWO."

Malka Risze thought she had prepared herself, but how could she? The lullaby her mother used to whisper to her became garbled; the gentle caress from her husband (she still called him her husband, even after all these years), now as faint as thin air; the faces of her son and daughter, jerky and pixelated.

Ramona said to those who were standing in front of her "Remove her filthy clothes from her" and Ramona told Malka "Look, I removed the dirt from you, and I will dress you with a fine robe" (Zech. 3:4).

Malka had still been able to hear those comforting words while being uncovered. She thought of her husband, she could never say her late husband, when Ramona celebrated Malka's body by washing it tenderly and chanting in Spanish, as if at church. Malka did not understand Spanish but was moved by the resonance of the lyrics, and she substituted words that she knew by heart:

His head is like the finest gold. His locks are curled and black as a raven.
Ramona poured water on Malka's head.

His eyes are like doves by the brook, bathing in milk, sitting at the border.
Ramona delicately washed Malka's closed eyes.

His cheeks are like a bed of spices, tower of perfume.
His lips are roses dripping with flowing myrrh.
And Malka felt a faint kiss from her husband, lightly against her lips.

His body is like polished ivory inlaid with sapphires.
It was not Ramona anymore who was gently brushing her body with pure water; it was Shimon, her husband.

His legs are pillars of marble set upon foundation of fine gold.
His appearance is like Lebanon, as select as the cedars.
She had never seen the famed cedar trees of Lebanon, but she remembered the tall pine trees of her neighborhood in Jerusalem, which were as majestic as their northern cousins.

His mouth is most sweet and he is altogether delightful.
And it was Sándor's, as she would call him on occasions when they spoke the old language during intimacy.

This is my beloved and this is my friend, daughters of Jerusalem (Cant. 5:11 – 5:16).

Malka had participated in the purification ritual with the sisterhood of her synagogue. The first time, she was shocked by the carnal sensuality of the Song of Songs spoken in this setting. She knew well the rabbis' commentaries. They had obliterated the corporeality of the Song of Songs by replacing its sensuality with an allegory of the love between God and the people of Israel, with Israel taken as His female counterpart. Malka remembered reading that same passage through the lens of the classic medieval commentary of Rashi, where the parts of the human *body* were transposed into parts of the divine *word*:

His head: His opening *words*.
His locks: His *crown*, holding mounds of *statutes*.
His eyes: His *eyes* are fixed on the waters of *Torah*.

His cheeks: His *words* at Sinai.
His lips: His comforting *words* from the Tabernacle.
His body: *The tablets* of the *Ten Commandments*.
His legs: *The Torah's* columns.
His mouth: *The words* of His palate.

  The reclaimed erotic rawness of the Song of Songs during
the purification ritual was even more shocking to Malka
because it was performed for a lifeless body, a corpse lacking
sensual and erotic qualities, a body being dressed in white
garments – like those worn by the Grand Priest for the Holy
of Holies – for its final journey. The daring reinterpretation
of the scriptures was not confined to the sensuality of the
body. In a clever collage of verses, tending to the deceased
became an allegory for God purifying the people of Israel,
and the allegory merged with Rashi's commentary on Song of
Songs. It was a secret ritual never discussed except among the
members of the Holy Society, the *Hevra Kadisha*, charged with
the *tahara*, the ritual purification of the deceased. Even the
membership to the Holy Society was to be kept a secret,
something that Malka was not supposed to disclose. Tending
to the deceased was seen as the ultimate act of charity, an act
which could never be repaid by its beneficiary. The secrecy
was, presumably, necessary to avoid bragging about this act
of *hesed*. However the secrecy protected also a most daring
interpretation of the scriptures: Tending to the corpse as a
sensual allegory for God's love. The body of the deceased
was, allegorically, at the same time the female partner of God,
and the people of Israel waiting to be purified by God. The
body represented also the Torah itself. The same Hebrew
word *aron* described the casket and the Ark of the Covenant
containing the tablets of the Ten Commandments which
were placed in the Holy of Holies, the inner sanctuary of the
Jerusalem Temple. Malka had placed the body in the casket,
while reciting a passage from the Bible relating the wrapping
of the Ark of the Covenant in the desert:

And they shall not come to see the wrapping of the Holy, lest they die (Num. 4:20).

The body represented the ultimate, seemingly heretical, secrecy, not only of the female consort in the holy couple of God and His beloved people, but also (could Malka say it?) of God Himself and His Torah. The members of the Holy Society were not only cleaning the body of the deceased, as if it were being prepared for the holy service in the Holy of Holies, they were also cleansing the community of Israel, the female consort of God, and her male counterpart, in preparation for their divine union. The continuous pouring of water was associated with the ritual bath, the *mikve*, the reservoir purifying the body of men and women, and of the bride before going to the wedding canopy.

Malka was afraid that she might not be granted this last sacred ritual. She had heard of morgues being over capacity and, as a result of this, cremation was sometimes required, against the family's wishes. She had kept a small package of earth from Mount Olive, from her volunteer work at the Jewish burial society. Traditionally, some of the earth of the Holy Land was sprinkled in the casket. The package had started to leak but a good amount of earth was still there and she put it in a small, sealed, clear plastic bag in order to preserve it. If she had to go to the hospital, she planned to put this bag in her pocket, and maybe it would stay with her in a temporary mass grave, until there could be a proper burial. She had wanted to be buried in Israel, next to her husband, but that was now an impossible dream, a dream from another time, from a time far away. She knew that cremation was a meaningful ritual for some people in in India and for some people in America. But for her, it was associated with the passing of many family members during the Shoah, including a grandmother she barely remembered, sent in her old age to Auschwitz.

Ramona continued to wash her frail body, the water dripping on the floor. Malka had heard that dripping before. Instead of the ancient myrrh fragrance, or the lavender perfume of the lotion Ramona was applying, Malka was overwhelmed by the stinging smell of the sewers. Drip, drip, drip... The dripping would not stop for hours, for days. Drip, drip, drip... – in the pitch dark, with no separation between day and night, between the water above and the water below, between the holy and the profane, between the sins of the dead and of the living. They had managed to find a dry area, large enough that she, her mother, and her little brother could even lie down in it and... wait. Wait for the food to come. Wait for clean water, for steps approaching with a flashlight. And she would try to recognize the splashy steps. Were they friendly or were they hostile? *Keep quiet. Shhh*, mother would whisper, hugging her more tightly; *Shhh*, when mother was scared. When she heard dogs trained to search for Jews hiding in the sewers, she would hug Malka to her chest, too tightly and for too long. Malka knew she could not complain, even if she was having difficulty breathing. Malka was not sure what panicked her the most: German dog barks echoing in the sewer, barely being able to breathe in her mother's chest-crushing embrace, or the terror her mother couldn't help but spread to them, clenching her teeth and her children together.

Gasping for air.
That was Malka's fear.
A fear aroused by a dog's bark.
A loving mother
Smothering her
Out of fear

Asthma attacks were bringing back memories. Once, at a synagogue board meeting, she started gasping for air. Instead of alerting the board members, among whom was a practicing physician, she left the meeting and went to hide in her office

71

in the dark. After a while the board members wondered where their rabbi had gone, and they found her breathing laboriously in her desk chair holding her arms tightly. Once she received medical attention and came back to her senses, the doctor asked her why she had left the boardroom at the beginning of an asthma attack. All she could answer was that *she had to.*

Ramona had stopped coming, but Malka was still reliving the precious washing and chanting. How could she prepare herself? Maybe she would remember good moments, like when she used to run in the grass after her little brother before the times of torment? Or when mother would sing to her before she went to sleep, *Oyfn Veg Shteyt A Boym*, the story of a little birdy trying to make its first flight from the nest, despite the burden of an overprotective mother. She could still see the humid eyes of her mother singing the last stanza:

Kh'hoyb di fligl, s'iz mir shver	*Heavy the wings, it's too hard*
tsu fil, tsu fil zakhn	*too many, too many things*
hot di mame ongeton	*has the mommy put on*
dem feygele, dem shvakhn.	*the little birdy, the weak.*
Kuk ikh troyerik mir arayn	*I look sadly, me, inside*
in der mames oygn	*in the mommy's eyes*
s'hot ir libshaft nisht gelozt	*her love didn't let*
vern mir a foygl.	*me become a bird.*

And she would have the same moist eyes when she sang the Yiddish lullaby to Rachel and Sammy.

Or her wedding day, waiting for Shimon to unveil her? She was pretty then. He had always been handsome in her eyes. Or after she first gave birth to her daughter Rachel, when she was given this little wrinkled package of love with the print of a right foot fitting on the back of her hand. Or simple moments, when they finally were safe enough to emerge from

72

the sewer. After getting used to the bright light, she was surprised by the fresh air filling her lungs, by the sharpness of the leaves way above her, by the shadow and the sun chasing each other like children in a playground while the breeze, passing through her, wiggled the leaves up the tree. Or when Shimon was sitting, as excited as she was, in the front row for her ordination at the Seminary, and maybe her parents were there too, somewhere, her father who would have been so proud of her, and her mother who would have approved of her no matter what.

Or she would turn to the scriptures for comfort.

"When you will raise the lights, the seven lights will illuminate the face of the menorah" (Num. 8:1-2). The lights are the human souls yearning to join their creator. Her light, her human soul, was yearning to illuminate the face of the creator of all lights, to unite with the One who said, let there be light, and there was light. Did God need His creatures? Yes, God was in search of the human soul, and the collective of human souls was the feminine divine presence yearning to join Him. And her light was about to illuminate His presence.

Gasping for air.

It was too late for the lights. For Yiddish, press "ONE." For English, press "TWO."

Isolation. Her beloved husband was not here. Even Sammy was not here. Rachel had not been talking to her for a long time. Malka, like her own mother, must have smothered her, and Rachel kept her distance. No visitor was allowed. A phone call maybe. Maybe now she would reconcile, finally, with Rachel.

Gasping for air.

For Yiddish, press "ONE." For English, press "TWO." The nurse dialed "ONE" for the recorded message of comfort from the absent chaplain. And she would recite her final prayer.

Shema Israel
Listen Israel
God is
Our God
God
is

9 Commentary on "ONE"
The Story of Malka Risze

Although never spelled out, the narrative titled "ONE" is written with reference to the COVID-19 pandemic of early 2020: the pulmonary symptoms, the overcrowded morgues, the threat of cremation against the wishes of the family, the isolation, the forbidden visits, and even the virtual chaplain.[9] There are also clearly references to the Holocaust, including Malka remembering when she was a little girl hiding in a sewer during the war. She would have been maybe 5 or 10 years old at the time, which would make her around 80 or 85 years old at the beginning of the pandemic.

Malka imagines herself dying of COVID, gasping for air. She appears to be suffering from some form of PTSD. That is, she is re-experiencing her time in the sewer when she hears the dripping water, and she seems to be having a flashback during her asthma attack.

Malka is trying to cope with the anticipation of her death, which she realizes is a daunting task:

---

[9] Sharon, 2020; Jerusalem Post Staff, 2020; Posner, 2020.

"Malka Risze thought she had prepared herself, but how could she?"

In the beginning of her story, she imagines three of her most fond memories accompanying her in her last moments: her mother's lullaby, her husband's caress, and her children's faces. Three circles of family and sensing: hearing her mother, feeling her husband, seeing her children.

Malka then backtracks to the time when Ramona used to wash her frail body. The description is vivid, as if it is happening now; however, it comes out in the story that Ramona had stopped coming to wherever Malka is in the present. We are left with two ways to understand this. Either the description of Ramona is from the past, and later on Malka is recalling it in the present tense; or Ramona is still coming regularly to care for Malka and Malka is anticipating losing Ramona.

Most likely, the isolation of a symptomatic COVID-19 patient described later, with a nurse and a chaplain (even an absent one) in an institution, points to a hospital setting. Her projection of herself into the future and into the past, and all these visions merging into a present narrative is an essential feature of the story.

We are thrown back further into a time when Malka was in good health when she, as member of the burial society in charge of the ritual cleansing of the body of the deceased, was in the caregiver role that Ramona has now. From there, Malka is anticipating her future, and her fear that she will not receive this meaningful ritual. She relives in the present the memory of actively performing the ritual cleansing, and imagines being herself the recipient of that ritual in the future. By replacing the impossible physicality of the ritual purification with words, Malka is paradoxically reversing the embodiment of the Song of Songs during the ritual cleaning, back into *words* through her story, almost returning to the

76

traditional allegoric interpretation of Rashi. The story itself and its words have the power to alleviate her fear of losing the physical ritual. In a way, Malka is cleansing herself in her mind, and preparing her body and mind for her last journey. With only one difference: she is aware of the powerful mystical associations of the ritual while she is experiencing it, unlike when it happens in reality. These associations help her connect with her husband in her yearning to unite with him. Those mystical associations are comforting and relieve her anguish about death. This fantasy writing has the therapeutic value of reframing her life and preparing her for the next stage.

Malka is giving us the clue of a symbolic object which could comfort her: a bag of earth connecting her with the Jewish burial ritual and with the land of Israel. We need to hear those clues, and see if it is feasible to grant her the simple wish of keeping that object with her. Otherwise, the story and the power of Malka's words would have to figuratively accompany her in her pocket, and substitute for the little bag of earth.

The story then switches, like a flashback, to the dark memory of her childhood in the sewer, connecting her current fear of not being able to breathe with her traumatic childhood experience. Malka is informing us about the meaning of her symptoms when she has an asthma attack, and of her fear of having those symptoms recur. Their symbolic meaning is unique to Malka, although the fear of being cremated is likely shared by other holocaust survivors.

Malka consciously tries to cope by anticipating that, during her final journey, she would remember the comforting moments of her life. Most of those moments are connected with important people in her family: her brother, her mother, her husband, and her children. She recalls the lullaby sung by her mother. That song connects generations of women, her mother and herself as a mother with her own daughter, generations of overprotective Jewish women singing the last stanza while almost crying. The last sentence *(her love didn't let me become a bird[10])* is heralding the distress of her unfinished business with her daughter, which is Malka's last anticipated thought. Her daughter has kept her distance because Malka was a smothering mother (figuratively), like her mother may have been (both physically and figuratively) and possibly her maternal grandmother, if we follow the hint of her mother's wet eyes.

Malka's connection with her religion is an important source of comfort, meaning, and recognition. She has become a Rabbi, a significant achievement, and she is applying her rabbinical knowledge to help herself. She pushes to the extreme the physicality of the Song of Songs as reinterpreted by the burial society, and returns to the literal meaning of the text: a celebration of human love. The meaning of the purification process is double. As a former participant in that ritual, she is well aware that the ritual purification is an allegory for preparing her to meet her creator in the most holy state, like the Grand Priest in the Jerusalem Temple, and for a mystical union with God. In her imaginary narrative, Malka feels free to superimpose on each other the meanings of human love and Divine love.

Malka's narrative resonates with traditional Jewish mystical interpretations. We find a similar allegorical commentary in the *Degel Machaneh Ephraim*, composed sometime between 1770 and 1800, a classic Hasidic work by Rabbi Moshe Chaim

---

[10] From *By the Road Stands a Tree,* a Yiddish poem by Itsik Manger (1901-1969). Translation of last two stanzas by Daniel Rosen. "*Oyfn veg shteyt a boym* was written in the mid-1930s, when Manger lived in Warsaw. It was immediately set to music by an anonymous composer, and became a folk song." (Personal communication by David G. Roskies)

Ephraim of Sudilkov in Ukraine, a grandson of the Baal Shem Tov, the founder of Hasidism:

> *The Lord spoke to Moses, saying: Speak to Aaron and say to him, "When you will raise the lights, let the seven lights illuminate toward the face of the menorah."* (Num. 8:1-2).

When you will raise the lights. Meaning that when you want to elevate the souls of (the people of) Israel, also called "lights," as it is written: "The human soul is the light of God" (Prov. 20:27).

The seven lights will illuminate toward the face of the menorah (candelabra). Meaning that you should intend to elevate (those souls) in order for them to illuminate and, so to speak, cleave to the face of the *shekhinah* (the divine presence), which has the quality of the *menorah*.

The seven lights will illuminate. This is the totality of the souls of Israel, also called *bat sheva* (Bathsheba, literally: the daughter of seven).[11]

In this text, the Rabbi alludes to the Hasidic concept of *dvekut* (cleaving to the *shekhinah*), loosely translatable as *unio mystica* (mystical union). In her narrative, Malka goes a step further. She sees her soul as about to be cleaved to the *shekhinah*, the feminine aspect of God, and the *shekhinah* herself is yearning to unite with the masculine aspect of the divine. We went full circle, from a physical union between male and female humans, to a mystical union between the human soul and the divine, and finally to a union between the

---

[11] *Degel Machaneh Ephraim* (section *Beha'alotcha*). Original Hebrew text from www.sefaria.org (translation by Daniel Rosen):

וזה י"ל פי' הפסוק בהעלותך את הנרות היינו כשתרצה להעלות נשמות של ישראל המכונים בשם נרות כמ"ש נר ה' נשמת אדם אל מול פני המנורה יאירו שבעת הנרות היינו שתוראה להעלות שיאירו וידבקו אל פני השכינה כביכול שהוא בחי' מנורה יאירו שבעת הנרות היינו כללות נשמות ישראל המכונים בשם בת שבע

79

masculine and feminine aspects of the divine, a classic mystical eschatological preoccupation in kabbalistic and Hasidic teachings, which is supposed to bring redemption to the world.[12]

There is another difference between Malka's references to the souls being elevated into the *shekhinah* and the *Degel Machaneh Ephraim*. In the *Degel Machaneh Ephraim*, the lights are the souls of the people of Israel, while for Malka the souls are all the souls of all people, not only the Jewish.

According to Proverbs: "The human soul is the light of God." This is clearly a universalistic statement, contrary to its interpretation in the *Degel Machaneh Ephraim*. Malka, as a modern ordained Rabbi, did not feel the need to exclude non-Jews from her mystical worldview. Malka was at peace with Ramona's Christian spirituality and its expression in her Christian chanting while cleansing her. Malka was touched by the melodic poetry of Ramona's lyrics and she used them as a springboard for her own spirituality. Ramona was associated with the angel of God standing in front of the Grand Priest in the Prophet Zechariah's vision. In that biblical passage, acting as a protector against Satan, the angel cleanses the Grand Priest in preparation for the renewed service in the rebuilt Temple of Jerusalem. This protective Angel is named by Malka "Ramona." The loose translation of Zechariah (3:4) is feminized, and Ramona is seen as Malka's protecting angel, starting the purification ritual. That verse is traditionally recited toward the beginning of the *tahara*, the Jewish ritual purification of the deceased. If Malka holds Ramona in such high esteem, how could she deny that Ramona's soul was also the light of God; especially since, right in the next chapter of Zechariah, the same angel shows to the Prophet a vision of the gold menorah and its seven lights?

---

[12] See Idel (2005).

Malka tries, through this imaginative story, to find meaning, purpose and comfort in her death. Does she succeed? Or, should we rather ask, does Malka imagine that she will succeed in reassuring herself at her ultimate moment? The answer is not clear. What is clear is her effort and her attempt.

"It was too late for the lights."

Does this mean that she had left behind the undemanding stage of being able to dwell with comforting thoughts about the lights and their symbolic mystical meaning? Does this mean that now all she could do was concentrate on her breathing, gasping for air in solitude? What would she think in her last frightening moments in the absence of her loved ones? Maybe she could reconcile with her daughter, a phone call from her may come, and this unfinished business could finally have some closure. But in this story, Malka does not find that closure. The lack of closure is symbolically marked by the absence of the last word in the recitation of the *shema*, the classic Jewish profession of faith uttered twice daily and just before dying. The full verse of the *shema* ends with the missing word "one":

"Hear, O Israel: the Lord is our God, the Lord is one." (Deut. 6:4)

What does the blank left by that missing "one" mean? Is this blank "nothing" an allegorical place left for the absence of God, symbolized also by the absent chaplain? Does this story finish as a macabre farce, where the protagonist ends up dying alone with no meaning given to her death? Was it like the fate of Maxim in *The Device*, who expires with neither Christian nor Jewish last rites, after an ironic and preposterous deal struck between a priest and a rabbi (Rosen, 2019, p. 24)? Or does this "nothing" represent Malka's leaping, as she has anticipated, into the Infinite, beyond words? Is she now under the protection of the divine "Nothing," the *"Ayin"* of the kabbalah?[13] Did Malka's light unite with the Holy One, blessed be He? Do the answers to these questions make a difference? In other words, is the process of writing what is most relevant here?[14]

The story does not end here. If we take at face value this visionary story as it is seen through Malka's eyes, she must still be alive to have told us her story. Through imagining her death, Malka concentrated on what was really important to her and what she felt she needed in order to find peace, and she discovered that this was her unfinished business with her daughter. Maybe it was not too late for her to call her daughter and have a resolution.

Using words, which serve as replacement for the loss of the ritual, Malka attempts to master her fear of this anticipated loss. She tries to give meaning to her life and her death through connection to her loved ones and to her faith, giving us clues to how to help her in this difficult time.

In this narrative, there are layers of fiction. The story of the anticipated fear is, of course, imagined. But it is imagined by Malka, the protagonist of the story who is herself also a fictional character. And the narrative voice of the story is in the third person, so the protagonist character could be an externalized version of a real-life Malka, or a literary creation of an author with a different biographical background. The power of fiction allows this revealing through concealment. In fact, I don't think I could have written about such a powerful fear in the first person. Malka, with her history, is

---

[13] Compare with the assertion in Tibetan Buddhism that at the point of death, the person experiences the true nature of consciousness, a "luminous emptiness" or "shining void" (Wicks, 1997).

[14] Bolton (2008) found that patients found the process of writing itself to be useful.

clearly different from me. As a child of a Holocaust survivor, I have experienced the Holocaust only indirectly. I have conducted in-depth interviews with more than a hundred Holocaust survivors. These interviews were for the German consulate in New York, starting in the late 1990s, for the evaluation of the survivors' disabilities secondary to wartime persecution (*Wiedergutmachung*). I have kept their stories vivid in my mind, and they were a source of inspiration for the character of Malka.

The imagined exposure to an anticipated trauma can help prepare for it, and integrate previous chaotic and fragmenting traumatic experiences. The story itself can foster connections by providing narrators with testimonies which can be witnessed and shared.

In Malka's narrative, her attempt to cope meaningfully with an anticipated trauma was shaped by her world view and her previous traumatic history. Narrators are better equipped to break their isolation and connect with their community by grounding their trauma narrative within a shared, culturally specific, symbolic language and history.

BIBLIOGRAPHY

Bolton, G. (2008). "Writing is a way of saying things I can't say"-therapeutic creative writing: a qualitative study of its value to people with cancer cared for in cancer and palliative healthcare. *Medical Humanities*. Vol.34(1), 40-46.
Idel, M. (2005): *Kabbalah and Eros*, Yale University Press: New Haven.
Jerusalem Post Staff. (2020) 'Final moments' prayer uploaded online for isolated coronavirus patients. *Jerusalem Post* (April 25). https://www.jpost.com/judaism/final-moments-prayer-uploaded-online-for-isolated-coronavirus-patients-625864 (accessed on July 7 2020).

Posner, M. (2020). Alone, COVID-19 Victims Hear Final Prayers Online. Hospital staff stand in for family and clergy. *Chabad.org/ news* (April, 22). https://www.chabad.org/news/article_cdo/aid/4720976/je wish/Alone-COVID-19-Victims-Hear-Final-Prayers-Online.htm (accessed on July 7 2020).

Rosen, D. (2019). *Butterfly Words: Relationships, A Psychiatrist's Narrative.* International Psychoanalytic Books, New York, NY.

Sharon, J. (2020). UK to give religious exemptions for cremation during coronavirus pandemic. *Jerusalem Post* (March 23). https://www.jpost.com/International/UK-Jews-worried-dead-may-be-cremated-due-to-coronavirus-pandemic-621997 (accessed on July 7 2020).

Wicks, R. (1997). The therapeutic psychology of The Tibetan Book of the Dead. *Philosophy East and West*, Vol.47(4), 479-494

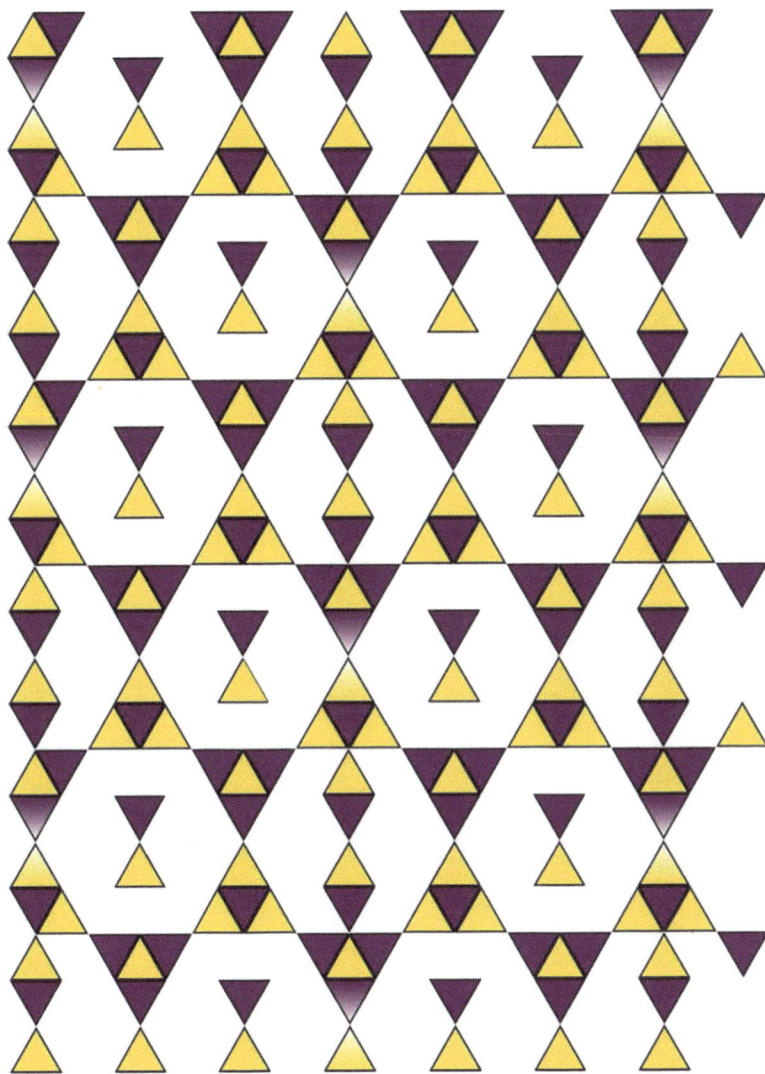

10 Ancestral Merit

Tinef. Written in simple but elegant font on its face:

Tinef

The letters were faint but still visible. A curious brand name. The hands were still moving. Maybe it was still working?

- *Combien?*
- *Deux cents Francs, Mademoiselle.*

Two hundred Francs! That was a lot, of course. It was not a bargain; it was a starting price for bargaining.

- *C'est une bonne Tinef.*

"It is a good Tinef!" Why did that arouse an indistinct memory for her?

In this small booth at the Marché aux Puces of St Ouen, she listened attentively to the merchant, who liked to talk.

It turned out that the merchant had bought the watch, sometime after the war, from an old Hungarian Jew. The merchant told her about the bad luck he'd had with that watch, wherever he would put it, nothing near it would sell. So he decided to leave it by itself in a corner of his small shop, to save his business. Who was this old Jew? The merchant didn't know. He was probably a Holocaust survivor

87

who may have found the watch in Budapest. The merchant remembered schmoozing with this old Jew and his strange accent, pronouncing his "a" almost like an "o," and telling him, in an encouraging tone: *"Monsieur Beheyme, C'est une bonne Tinef."*

"The bear and the cow will live in peace together." This quote from Isaiah in Hebrew accompanied a miniature painting of a stuffed cow and bear on the border of the parchment. They must have cherished those stuffed animals as pets to play with, as some childless couples do. After a while, it must have been time to advance their engagement to the real thing, and maybe they kept the animals as a messianic symbol, a good omen for their growing relationship. A watch was displayed in the center of the bottom border, next to the miniature paintings of a flower with its brilliant shade of gold, and of a croissant dipped into a cup of hot chocolate. On the face of the watch was written in very small Hebrew letters:

טנוף

– Who gave you that, Mr Beheyme?
– Funny you should ask, Mademoiselle, but it is the same old Jew who sold the watch to me. This is a genuine Jewish marriage contract, a *ketubah*. By the way, my name is Bensaïd.
– Are you Jewish?
– Mademoiselle, in Paris we don't ask the question this way. Let's say that I can read each letter "tet, nun, waw, feh," but I don't know how to read the word.

The merchant had a North African Arabic accent when talking in French and when pronouncing the Hebrew letter "waw." Maybe he was just a good businessman who made the effort to learn how to recognize the 22 letters of the *Aleph-Bet*, or maybe he was a Jew who preferred to remain discreet about his origins. In New York, the question would have been answered straightforwardly with a yes or a no. But here,

88

when on vacation antiquing in a flea market north of Paris, it was, apparently, a touchy subject.

– *Combien?*
– Are you Jewish?
– I thought you were not supposed to ask.
– You are right. Would you take a cup of freshly made mint tea?

Now Hannah knew they were getting down to serious bargaining. If she let on that she was Jewish, he would ask more for the parchment. And if she revealed that she could read the Hebrew letters and knew how they were pronounced with a Yiddish accent like the brand name of the watch, he would want to charge her even more. If they both acknowledged that they were Jewish, this might create a bond which would make it hard for her to leave without buying something or at least continuing to bargain with him for a while.

– This is a unique piece which is easily worth 1000 Francs, but for you, because you are such a nice girl, I will give it to you for 500 Francs.
– "With the watch?" she asked, while sipping the hot tea.

She realized it had been a mistake to accept the honey-sweetened tea, but she hadn't been able to resist. It would make the price negotiation more difficult, but *tant pis*, she hadn't tasted such a good mint tea since she visited the souk in Marrakesh.

Hannah needed to know more. Could he find the old Jew? She could sense Monsieur Bensaïd's concern about revealing his sources, but with her nice smile and some cajoling—she was a lovely young woman, after all—and after paying a good price for the lot, he gave her the contact information for the old Jew.

II

Moïse Katzman was, as usual, at the workbench in his printshop on the Rue des Rosiers when Hannah entered the store which had samples of invitation cards for weddings and bar-mitzvahs displayed in its windows. Showing him her watch, she asked:

– What does *tinef* mean?

She already knew the answer. She had stopped by the bookstore around the corner, facing the oldest – "SINCE 1946" – Jewish bakery in the *pletzel*, as the Jewish quarter in Le Marais section of Paris was affectionally called. In a Yiddish dictionary she had found:

> Yiddish טנוף (tinef), from Hebrew טִנּוּף (tinnúf, "trash")
> 1. dirt, filth
> 2. dung, excrement
> 3. junk, stuff of poor quality
> 4. incapable person, good-for-nothing

Who on earth would name a watch brand *Junk*?

The shopkeeper could not resist breaking into a big laugh.

– Where did you get it? Did you buy it from Monsieur Beheyme? It was so long ago, I'd almost forgotten all about it.
– Monsieur Bensaïd.
– Whatever. Did you also get the *ksube*?

She knew the Yiddish pronunciation for *ketubah*.

90

– Yes. Why do you call him Monsieur Beheyme? What did you mean by telling him "It is a good tinef?" Where did you get these?
– *Madame, vous allez trop vite.*

Now, with him, she was a *lady* who was *going too fast*, not a "Mademoiselle." No chance of flirting with this short old man, with his white beard and thick glasses. He was barely even looking at her. Hannah knew it would take time to uncover the story. Her story.

III

A man in complete Hungarian peasant attire, down to his boots, walked into the jewelry store in Miskolc, a county capital in northern Hungary. Each time the door opened, the cold winter wind penetrated for a moment. David had stood by this door for many years as an apprentice jeweler, suffering mutely from the sudden chill each time anyone entered or left the store. They were long years. But one day his boss decided to retire. And David surprised him: He had carefully saved every cent he could and so had enough to buy the store. Now he was sitting at the counter away from the door when he greeted the peasant who had come to buy a watch. David routinely used the formal Hungarian greeting *szervusz*, "at your service."

– *Szervusz*, Mr. Beheyme, what about this watch? It's a good Tinef.

The peasant responded in Yiddish. They both laughed and became friends. Of course, had David known that the seemingly non-Jewish Hungarian peasant was actually a Jew,

91

he would never have called him Mr. Beheyme (*Mr Beast*, in Yiddish), and he would have avoided the Tinef watches. David had bought those junk watches by weight and decided to brand them in Yiddish for what they really were: pieces of *junk*. David, a self-made modern man at the beginning of the 20th century, had left his shtetel in the Carpathian Mountains at the age of 13. After his bar-mitzvah, as the youngest son of a large and poor Hasidic family, his father told him that he was now an adult man and placed him as apprentice in Miskolc so he could earn a living. This harsh decision probably saved David's life by moving him out of a shtetel destined to be liquidated toward the end of WWII.

Was David to be blamed for using that not so innocent insider joke with non-Jews? By today's standard yes, but then in an anti-Semitic Hungary – who knows?

Later on, David moved to Budapest where he became a successful jeweler. He had two jewelry shops on Váci utca, the most exclusive and elegant street of jewelers in Budapest at the time, more the equivalent of la Rue de la Paix in Paris than 47th street in New York. After a client visited one store, the staff would call the other store and alert them about who the client was and what the client was looking for, so that they could be prepared and could do a better job of selling.

David became an expert at appraising diamonds. In November 1934, when he became an official auctioneer for the Hungarian government tasked with selling jewelry repossessed by the state, he was required to exchange his Jewish-sounding last name for a good Hungarian-sounding name. Though the Hungarian State was more than ready to make a profit by employing such a qualified Jew, this could not be done openly.

The deal was simple. The official auctioneer would set the price for the jewelry, and he would have to buy what did not sell, but at a 5% discount. David, knowing the exact worth of the jewelry, would set the price a little above its value, and would buy for his own shops what did not sell at the auctions.

This was legal. But was it ethical? Maybe it was murky in the same way that it was murky to advertise a junk watch as "a good Tinef."

IV

– **D**o you know how fast you were driving? You didn't see me? I was right behind you!

Tom answered the young woman in a gray uniform and large yellowish hat, who walked up to his window after pulling him over on the highway:
– 55?
– No. 75. Do you know what the speed limit is?
– 50. Sorry I was distracted; I'm on my way to work.
– Do you know how many points that'll be on your license? A lot. Stay in the car.

Tom had been rushing to work while making a phone call on his hands-free cell and had not noticed the obvious State Police car driving behind him on the almost empty highway. The cute police officer went back to her car, no doubt to check his record. He did not have a record of felonies or speeding tickets. Maybe she would just give him a warning? He had never driven so fast, at least not on this highway.

Now Tom was getting even more late for work, while she was checking her computer with her partner in the police car.

He began opening the door to talk to her, but she sent a stern warning over the loud speaker:

– SIR, STAY IN THE CAR!

So he waited, and waited. Maybe they were talking about letting him go? Would his license be suspended? How would he get to work? Would he have to go to court?

When she approached his car again, his window was already down from before, when she had pulled him over.

– Today is your lucky day. The computers are down. You should drive slower.

She said this firmly but softly, and without a smile, while returning his license and registration.

Tom recalled a class he had taken once about ancestral merit. The cute police officer was not lying about the computer being down. It wasn't that she had fallen for him or decided to just give him a warning because he had no previous record. This must have been his *zekhut avot*, his ancestral merit. Now he himself had to perform some good deeds in order to replenish his merit. This driving episode must have cost him quite a few points in his *zekhut avot* account. Of course Tom was glad to have escaped the consequences of his driving mistake although he was worried to have wasted some of his *zekhut avot* for something so trivial, instead of keeping it in reserve for a time of grave physical danger in the midst of persecution. Tom smiled at this worry. He was not so naïve to believe that his *zekhut avot* was a piggy bank, an account he could draw from when in need, or like having spiritual overdraft protection. But still, he knew that his ancestors had suffered during the Shoah, often paying with their lives, and they had left bundles of accumulated merit for him, their only surviving relative.

V

– So why was it so bad to eat the forbidden fruit from the tree of knowledge? We would not want lose our ability to know the difference. Isn't this what makes us human adults? Who would not want to know about good and evil? A child, or a feeble spirit. If the Garden of Eden is a paradise for children, don't we want to grow up and leave it, in order to know what is good or bad and struggle to do the right thing?

– God wanted us to eat that fruit, said Rabbi Jeremy. We passed the test. On the other hand, God did not want Abraham to sacrifice his son. Abraham failed the test.

– Is this radical theology, Rabbi?

– Maybe, Tom. Take Rabbi Nahman of Bratslav for example. He says that learning the code of Jewish law provides a great *tikkun* ("reparation"), purifying ourselves and repairing all the impairments we have caused by our sins, because the study of the codes enables us to distinguish properly the good from evil. And this knowledge is the essence of all reparations (*tikkuninm*).[15] From what Rabbi Nahman says, without eating from the fruit of knowledge between god and bad, we would not be able to perform any *tikkun*.

– Yes, but then we would not have any sin to repair!

– I guess the problem contained already its remedy. Look at the *Mei HaShiloach*, now this is radical theology:

---

[15] See: Lamm, Norman (1999): The religious thoughts of Hasidism: Text and Commentary. Yeshiva University Press, p 227.

"If he [Adam] had stayed in the Garden of Eden after the sin, he would have been able to repent completely and purify himself entirely. However God wanted that this sin would not be purified until later, so that all the generations after him would be able to have the merit of their good deeds being attributed to them. For this he was expelled from the Garden of Eden."[16]

— This is quite different from the Christian doctrine of the original sin!

— God delayed the *tikkun* of that sin, in order for the later generations to have merits and perform reparations (*tikkunim*) on their own. This means that performing those reparations through good deeds is what God wants for humankind. This is as close as possible to saying that eating the fruit of the tree of knowledge was a good thing.

— I never knew that you could interpret the story of the first sin this way! Rabbi, could the merits of good deeds be passed between generations?

— Yes Tom, and they can be passed both ways. Not only from ancestors to children but also from children to ancestors.

— Both ways?

— Yes, and not only can the good deeds benefit the children, even till a thousand generations, but also the not so good

---

[16] Rabbi Mordechai Yosef of Izbicy (1801-1854): *Mei HaShiloach*, Volume 2 (*likutim*) at the end of his commentary on Genesis. Original Hebrew text from www.sefaria.org (translation by Daniel Rosen):

ואם היה עוד אחר החטא בגן עדן היה יכול לעשות תשובה בשלימות ולברר עצמו לגמרי, ורצון השי"ת היה שהחטא לא יתברר עד לעתיד, כדי שכל הדורות אחריו יסגלו מעשים טובים שיהיו נקראים על שמם, לכן נתגרש מגן עדן

deeds in need of *tikkun* can be passed, to a lesser extent, up to the third or fourth generation.[17]

– I understand that we can draw from the merit of our ancestors, Abraham, Isaac and Jacob, but ultimately aren't we judged by our own deeds? Can we help previous generations?

– This is what reciting the mourner's *Kaddish* is about. Through the good deed of reciting the *Kaddish*, the relative helps the soul of the departed. According to the Zohar, children's good deeds in the physical word ensure that their father can silence the accusations of the angels and enter the world to come.[18]

– So, Rabbi, it is possible to perform some *tikkun* for a dead relative?

– According to the tradition, yes. There is a back-and-forth relationship between the generations. Tom, what's on your mind?

– I don't know, Rabbi. I may have some repair work to do. I am not sure.

– What do you mean?

– It has to do with watches, especially nice watches. All I can keep are junk watches. The nice ones are lost, taken away from me, or in need of expensive repair.

– Did you do the repair?

---

[17] Exodus 20:5-6

[18] Zohar I,115a-115b. See: Tishby, Isaiah (1989) *The wisdom of the Zohar: An Anthology of Texts.* Translated from Hebrew by David Goldstein. The Littman Library of Jewish Civilization: London, Washignton. Volume III, page 1406, note 263.

– No, it was not worth it.

– So now you want to do the *tikkun*?

– How do you do a repair for a watch, Rabbi?

– First, you have to find what the root of the problem is.

– Like a root cause analysis or ancestral therapy? And then?

– And then, Tom, you will have to be extra careful in the future about the spirit of the law which was broken or the ethical principles which had been disregarded, in order to repair that watch.

VI
A House

Today I bought a house
Ephemeral, of no significance
Today you fought as usual
It was too soon, you didn't have the time
Nothing much important
Today we bought a temporary house
Together
You were thinking of a future for it in your world
And me in mine
You would ask the board for next year
To put it in the backyard of your building
I thought I may take the house in two years
Ship it to Jerusalem and plant it in my garden
A house with conflicting expectations
A house for your life and a house for mine.
This year we bought a house together
A house of no consequence
A house for a week, for a weekend
A house to build
A house to dismantle
To disassemble, to break down
A perennial house, to rebuild again
This year with the kids
Next year apart
A house expandable
To grow with, to multiply for when we
You and I, you or I
Will have guests again
A house with no hope of becoming permanent
A house expendable, dispensable, disposable
Just a little play house

VII

Hannah wondered who was this couple who had put a junk watch on their *ketubah*? Was she related to them? According to Monsieur Bensaïd, the watch was not a good omen. She had vaguely heard those ironic and misleading words before: "This is a good Tinef!" Was it because of this sentence that they had put the Tinef watch on their marriage contract, as a connection with the ancestors? Had they known that a curse was attached to the watch? Most likely not; but the contract was flawed from its conception and the prosecuting angel must have held the *ketubah* as defective. Maybe the same prosecuting angel had heard a mispronounced word at the time of the wedding? Instead of hearing "You are now married to me according to the *law* (*dat* in Hebrew) of Moshe and Israel," the prosecuting angel heard "according to the *intention* (*daat* in Hebrew) of Moshe and Israel?" A long "aa" is a barely perceptible flaw which may have gone unnoticed by all the rabbis present at the ceremony, while being retained in the archives of this accusatory angel. The *ketubah's* drawing of the watch, was an unfortunate reminder that the "law" had been displaced by an inappropriate "intention," an intention contradicting the purpose of a marriage where the interest of the other should prevail over one's own. Did the marriage last or was it dissolved? If the marriage had lasted, wouldn't the *ketubah* have been carefully preserved in the family instead of ending up in a flea market? Had the divorced couple continued to see each other? Had they shared some meals with their children during the holidays, for a Passover dinner or for a meal during Sukkot? Did they cooperate enough to build the temporary dwelling of a Sukkah, even if they could not keep a permanent home together? Did he learn from his mistakes, and did she remarry? Did each of them finally find happiness ever after?

100

VIII

The Swiss Army symbol replacing the number 12 had fallen under the glass and got stuck under the big hand, preventing it from advancing. After Tom shook the band vigorously, the fluorescent white cross above its red background floated freely under the crystal. It would niche itself above the date display, or on one of the chronograph subdials, and would continue to obstruct the circulation of time. Tom tried to remove the crystal, but it was impossible, and he gave up looking for someone specialized in this sort of work. So, the repair project stayed in a drawer in Tom's night table for a while, and when was the moment to clean all the junk accumulated in this drawer, it was dropped in an unmarked storage box full of unneeded items which still had a certain value. The box was placed among other boxes in one of the storage areas, in the basement or on a high shelf in the butler's pantry. And Tom forgot about it.

– "But it is just a little plus symbol," argued Greg about the Red Cross insignia. "Why wouldn't the Magen David Adom, (the Israeli equivalent of the Red Cross) work under a red cross symbol when abroad?"

– For the same reason that Muslim countries work under a red crescent: it is a Christian cross, the reverse of the Swiss Flag and it probably comes from a crusader's flag. I still remember, when I was a kid, playing with toy soldiers from the crusades carrying their white shield with a big red cross on it. The crusaders persecuted Jews in Europe on their way to Jerusalem. Even now, math textbooks from religious schools in Israel avoid using signs resembling a cross and truncate the plus sign like this: ⊥.[19]

---

[19] See also: The Jewish Encyclopedia (1906), p. 369.

For years, Tom abstained from buying a Swiss Army watch because of its cross in its symbol, although he did carry his treasured Swiss Army knife, which he found very useful when in the woods. One day, though, he impulsively bought the expensive watch at the airport before boarding a Swissair plane. But apparently, he was not destined to wear it for long.

The story reminded him of the beautiful gold watch he, Mordechai grandson of David, had received for his Bar Mitzvah. A gorgeous, elegant real Swiss watch with its golden expandable wrist band.

– "This must be a very good watch," Mordechai's father, the son of David, had said. "Your grandfather was a jeweler who knew about watches. He must have chosen a good watch for you!"

Mordechai did not have the opportunity to take good care of it. A few days later, he flew back home with his parents after his Bar Mitzvah ceremony. He had worn the watch in the plane, happy about this gift. But when he looked for the time through the round glass held by the gold wristband, all he could see was the skin of his arm. The watch itself had disappeared. It must have fallen off. Or maybe it was retrieved by a malicious spirit who considered him an unworthy recipient of that gift. His father, instead of being angry, said something that marked the young Mordechai:

– Don't tell your grandfather, don't say anything.

And so, this little secret between Mordechai and his father, who wanted to protect his own loving father from feeling disappointed and obligated to buy another expensive watch,

---

http://www.jewishencyclopedia.com/articles/4776-cross

was all that was left from this wonderful Bar Mitzvah gift; a story replacing a lost heirloom.

Tom kept the useless gold bracelet for many years. Over time, the size of the bracelet had shrunk, or so it seemed, and Tom could not wear it anymore on his now stronger and bigger arm, even if he had found a watch to fit under the glass. He stored the gold bracelet in a closet, and placed it beside a gold ring inlaid with a small ruby, which had belonged to David, and which his grandfather used to wear on his little finger. But even this reminder of the gold watch, along with the gold ring, had disappeared, vaporized in time like the golden calf's pulverized pieces were dispersed in water by Moses when he returned from Mont Sinai. Tom had left the heirlooms in his empty bedroom at his widowed elderly mother's apartment, and an unscrupulous home aide, or maybe an accusatory angel, must made off with them.

When Tom thought about a Bar Mitzvah gift for his own son, Tzvi, he had wanted to give the only heirloom watch in his possession. A watch with 2 clocks for different time zones, a truly luxurious watch made of platinum which had belonged to his son's grandfather, Tom's father-in-law. His wife had given the watch to Tom after the passing of her father. But the wristband was too big, as it was fitted for the strong and long arms of his tall father-in-law. And so the watch sat unused on a shelf for a while, until Tom decided to have the wristband professionally adjusted, so that he could wear it before he would give it to his son. For his son would feel the love of generations of fathers, from both his father and his grandfather even if this grandfather was not the father of his own father. But when he looked for the watch, Tom could not find it. His wife at the time had taken the gift back before their divorce and she gave the grandfather's watch to their son, bypassing Tom. Had she imagined that Tom would withhold the heirloom watch from their son, or that it would be passed on to someone else? What did hurt him more was not that his son got the watch. It was his intention anyway to give it to Tzvi and repair the loss of his own grandfather's watch. Now, he could not buy a new gorgeous watch for his son, since Tzvi had already received one. What was stolen from Tom was not the double-faced platinum watch, but the possibility of giving a watch to his son, to pass on a family memento to be held onto for generations. All what Tom could pass on was a story of elegant watches, which were not completely lost, because they survived in memory through his story.

Tzvi was a teenager, difficult to please, and he had not worn his Bar Mitzvah watch even once. It was a mature adult watch, not fit for a teenager. Once, when on vacation, Tom found a trendy black watch, a little bit showy but of good taste, not garish or too flashy like what some street kids would show off with in the Bronx or in Brooklyn. Compared to his platinum grandfather's watch, it was junk. Not sure if Tzvi would approve, Tom gave it to him when he returned from his trip, without making a big deal of it. His son did not say much, but he apparently appreciated the gift, and Tzvi, who had never used one before, adopted the black watch and wore it every day.

New York,
October 8, 2020

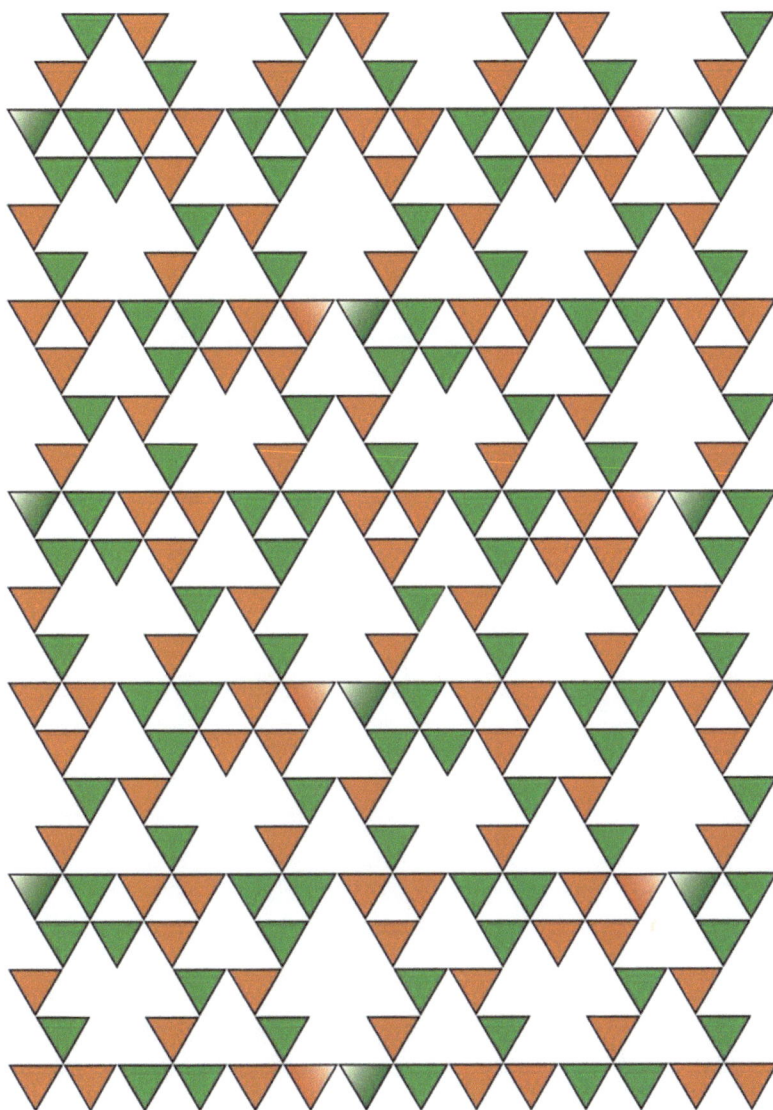

11 Looking for Paradise

The flood story can reveal the aspirations of humanity after the expulsion from paradise. What was the Garden of Eden? A place where all our needs were provided for, abundant food, a safe place to stay, a time when it is not shameful to be naked, when we don't know the difference between good and bad. It is the blissful idealized imagination of what childhood must have been like, before we knew how to differentiate between good and bad, between right and wrong. Of course we have to grow up and leave the Garden of Eden, when after eating the forbidden fruit, our eyes are opened, our awakening sexuality is represented by the snake with its obvious phallic symbolism. Even then, before the expulsion from this idyllic world, we are provided with clothes on our way out.

Sometimes we yearn to go backwards to this paradisiacal world when all was provided to us, or even further backward, back to the womb. This must be an ancient human fantasy. But with Noah, instead of God being the only actor who decided to put us in Eden and to expel us with the curse of sexuality, we, humans, will be in charge of leaving the paradise of the womb. This exit from paradise will even be accompanied, not by a sense of guilt and shame, along with God's wrath like in Eden, but by God's repeated blessing of our sexuality and our need to reproduce (Gen 9:1). The same blessing to be fruitful and multiply had already appeared before the eating of the forbidden fruit (Gen. 1:28). However, in the Garden of Eden, sexuality was associated with sin in the figure of the snake, with shame in the awareness of being naked, and finally resulted in the expulsion from paradise.

In Eden and in Noah's ark, all our needs are provided for, in a safe place. The ark could be compared to a womb

107

floating in amniotic liquid, protecting us from a dangerous world. However, while in the paradise story, we humans had nothing to do with coming into or leaving this protected place, in Noah's story, we, humans, are the actors, under God's guidance. We have to make the ark, we enter and leave the ark of our own volition, and we even have to feed the animals. The ark is a metaphor for a paradisiac protected space where the wolf and the lamb, the bear and the cow, live peacefully together, like in Isiah's messianic vision (Isa. 11:6-7). However, after such a long confinement and lockdown (the rabbis have calculated that it must have lasted a year), Noah must have been eager to leave the ark for an imperfect adult world of growth, labor and love, and with the blessing that animals will fear humankind. As did our ancestors, we may still fanaticize about this lost paradise. Noah himself used the produce of the vine to reach a temporary state of drunkenness where he forgot what was right from wrong, and was not ashamed of being naked.

There is a parallel between those two paradise stories and the two sets of tablets given to Moses at Sinai. The flood story repeats a sequence of the 40 days and 40 nights (Gen. 7:12 and 8:6), and this symbolic number reminds us of the 40 days and 40 nights Moses spent both times he was on Mount Sinai being fed only by the divine words (Ex. 24:18 and 34:28). In the first set of those two stories, the human receives nurturance from God passively, a physical nurturance in the Garden of Eden, and a spiritual nourishment with the tablets.

The first tablets provided to Moses were written by God's finger (Ex. 31:18), but they were not followed by the people, and the tablets were broken. Only the second set of tablets survived, when Moses partnered with God and engraved the tablets himself, presumably under God's guidance (Ex. 34:27-28). Similarly, from a symbolic point of view, the first story of the Garden of Eden describes the first incomplete process of growing up and leaving for the world. Only the second coming of age story, with Noah, is the process completed because it is a story with active human participation. Noah's partnership in his survival, to be sustained in life, prefigures the need for human partnership in God's word, the Torah, our spiritual sustenance.

This yearning to return to a mythic paradise, to the Garden of Eden, drives us to strive to recreate it here and now on earth. Did the ancients imagine Eden as the Hanging Gardens of Babylon, or the Sennacherib's gardens at Nineveh, with their marvels of man-made aqueducts? Was it recreated in the Alhambra gardens? Those magical gardens, like our gardens today, needed water. The Garden of Eden was watered by four confluent rivers; including the Euphrates in Mesopotamia and possibly the great Nile River, which was referred to as a river running around the land of Cush, perhaps through Ethiopia.

When Lot parted from Abraham (who was then still named Avram), he chose the valley of the Jourdan, well irrigated "like a Garden of God, like the land of Egypt" (Gen. 13.10). Lot had found his Garden of Eden. But he, like Adam, was expelled from it because of the violent (sexual) sins of its residents, who perished like Noah's contemporaries. In this retelling of a lost paradise, Lot's Garden of God was destroyed, through divine fire rather than water, and became the most desolate desert (Gen. 19:24).

The search for a lost paradise is not over. God makes a covenant with Abraham, through sexuality with the circumcision. The previous commandment to procreate is now repeated as a blessing of fertility, for innumerable descendants. God promises a new paradise to Abraham, the entire Fertile Crescent: "On this day, God established a covenant with Abraham by saying: 'I gave this land to your seed, from the river of Egypt to the big river, the river

Euphrates'" (Gen.15:18). This grand gift is in the next verse applied more strictly to the most arid part of the Fertile Crescent, the land of Canaan and other people. Abraham had just experienced a famine in this land and was forced to go to Egypt for sustenance (Gen. 12:10). Nevertheless, the Promised Land is symbolically framed by the two largest rivers of this ancient world, including at least one, and maybe two, of the rivers irrigating the original Garden of Eden. This Promised Land is an attempt to recreate the lost paradise for Abraham and his descendants, like Lot had tried near the Jordan River.

The idea of a divine garden may be found in Sumerian texts, according to Samuel Noah Kramer.[20] This ancient quest for a Garden of Eden continued with the Jerusalem Temple, which had been interpreted as a recreation of God's garden.[21]

In our days of confinement from the flood of the viral storm out there, we, like Noah, are taking an active role to protect ourselves, our community and all humankind, and we continue to care for each other. This flood too will pass and, in the meantime, we do our best to continue our active participation in our spiritual sustenance, also looking, like our ancestors to make earth a sustainable Garden of Eden.

New York,
October 21, 2020

---

[20] Kramer, Samuel Noah (1964). The Sumerians: Their History, Culture and Character. University of Chicago Press. p. 293.
[21] See for example: https://reformedforum.org/summarizing-biblical-theological-case-eden-temple-garden/

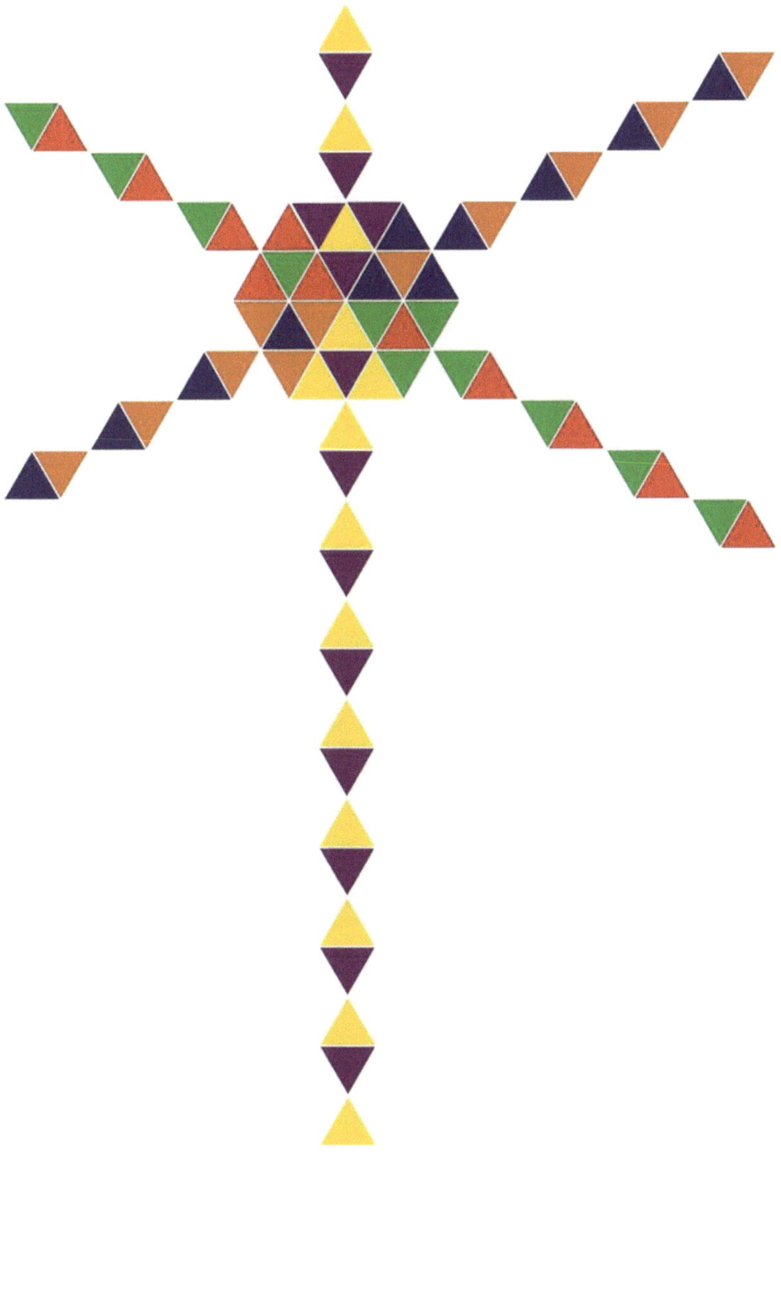

12 Hallelujah

In the Garden of Eden a bright light shines above the green grass dotted with roses. Greek sculptures and tall white candles stand like columns planted in the grass. Here, in heaven, we joined our souls in Holy Matrimony. Joseph is Egyptian, so for our wedding on earth I would wear a red dress like a Gypsy, to honor his origins. We gave each other the pledge six and a half years ago and we have not met since. A few weeks ago it finally happened. I rose to heaven in my dream, found Joseph in the Garden of Eden and married him. But they would not let me. They attacked me with their *twenty-one of vision*, to destroy God. They also attacked my daughter Tina because they knew how I love her. Through her, they hoped to destroy me and prevent me from bringing Baby Jesus back to the world, the baby I would get from my husband Joseph. When I learned that my own mother, Rebecca, planned to prepare spare ribs for dinner for Tina, I called my daughter straightaway to warn her not to eat any of that food. My mother did not usually cook; there was only one reason for that dinner: to poison Tina through the *twenty-one of vision*. My mother's cousins were also conniving with her, and so was my boyfriend Ethan, or, rather, my ex-boyfriend. We had not had sex since I married Joseph in Holy Matrimony. Ethan attacked me through the *twenty-one of vision*. I had to defend myself. I had to protect God, Baby Jesus, so I broke Ethan's arm. But now, although I want to beat up the sinners, I won't use violence. Besides, I do not want to go to jail. I heard that Ethan's pressed charges and a warrant has been issued for my arrest. Earlier, I had wished for Ethan to visit me, only to punish him and punch him. But now I would let God take care of it. Instead, I used White Magic to counter their Black Magic. I recited many times *Ave Maria* and *Pater Noster*. My prayers were answered and God took the power away from the *twenty-one of vision*. Despite their evil intention, the sinners could not destroy the world. They will not prevent my spiritual impregnation by Joseph and the birth of Baby Jesus. I will call him Kaiser, but I would know that in reality his name was Jesus. There are many sinners in the world. The Pope will burn in hell because he supports gay marriage. I carry a newspaper clipping of an article describing the Pope's position, along with another clipping of an article showing pictures of Hasidic Jews and a copy of the Koran. You see the curls on those Jews? If we put them up, they look like horns. They are the Devil. They will burn in hell. I'm following the religion of God. I read the story of Joseph in the Koran. I want to make you a beautiful yarmulke with shiny white pearls all around it, in a circle. My family will also burn in hell. My uncle touched me when I was six. It was not really abuse because there was no penetration. My grandfather beat him up. My mother knew. She will also burn in hell. She abused me emotionally. Jews paid a lot of money for my family to sell me to get raped. The man who pretended to be my father was not my real father. My father was an Arab, like Joseph. My mother once cut the hands off all the statues of the many shrines she had at home. This scared me. My grandmother has performed witchcraft since I was a child. They would meet in a circle but they would not let me in. I was like a stranger to them. Sorry, but I need to leave. I have to get ready for Halloween. I don't care about the ghosts. It is just a fun holiday. I bought a costume. I will be Superwoman. I need to do my hair, otherwise I would look like a witch.

She pressed her fingers through her long, thick yellowish hair. Here comes the Devil, she says jokingly when a Jewish man with no curls enters the room. I am OK now. I am not going to break anybody's arm. Let me go home. I will be safe. There is no more witchcraft. In the battle against evil, God won. Hallelujah.

New York,
October 28, 2020

114

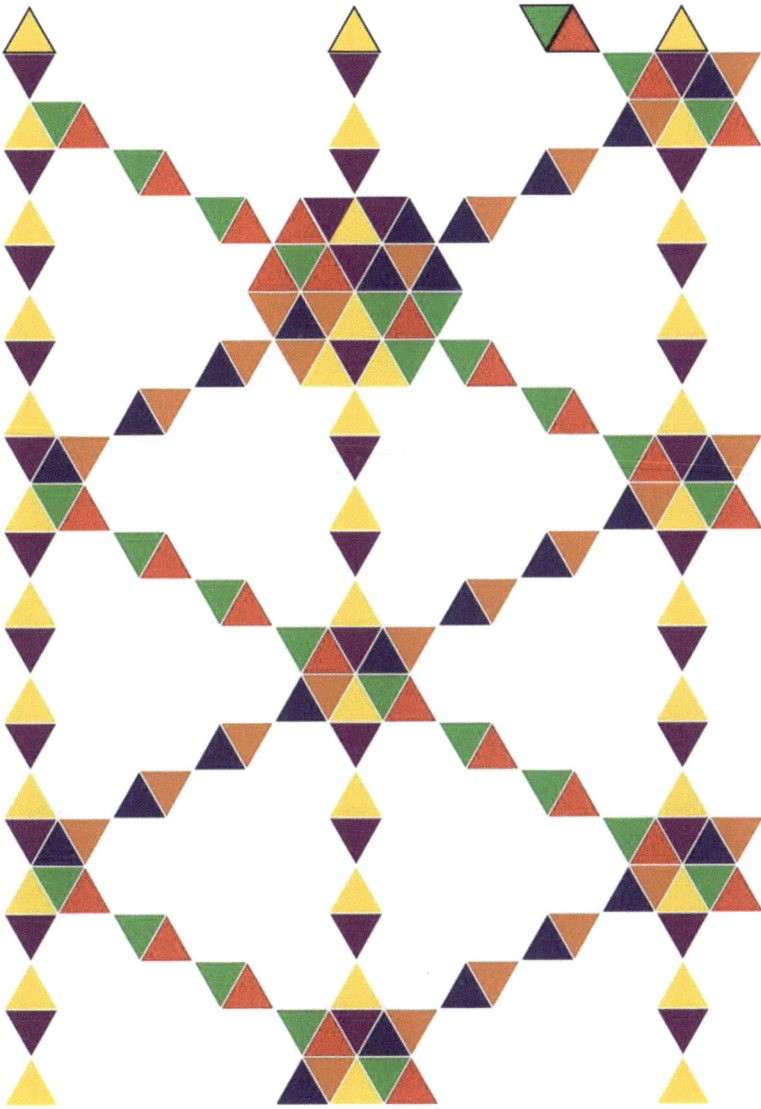

13 The Binding of Isaac

We need to look at Hammurabi's Code to resolve the fundamental ethical question raised by the story of the Binding of Isaac (Gen. 22:1-19): How could Abraham be so eloquent and forceful with God when fighting for the survival of Sodom (Gen. 18:23-33) and then, later, be so submissive, not saying a word, when told by God to sacrifice his own son? Abraham also does not say a word against letting his other son, Ishmael, be sent to his death in the desert, after God tells Abraham to listen to his wife Sarah (Gen. 21:11-14). Not only does Abraham listen to God, in both cases, he also does not drag his feet, but gets up early in the morning, so eager is he to obey God's commands, commands which will result in the deaths of his sons. (Gen. 21:14 and 22:3).

Similarly, we find the attitude of Lot shocking. While Abraham is praised for his generosity when welcoming the three strangers passing by his tent (Gen. 18:1-8), Lot does much more: he closes his door behind him, going out to confront the angry mob of Sodom, clearly placing his life in danger to save his visitors from being sexually assaulted (Gen. 19:6), something Abraham did not have to do. We understand the request of the people of Sodom as being sexual in nature when they ask Lot to release his three visitors so that they might "know" them, in the biblical sense (Gen. 19:5). Instead, Lot offers his two virgin daughters to the visibly excited crowd, for the men to do what they will with the girls, in exchange for the safety of the visitors (Gen. 19:8). What?

According to Hammurabi's Code (Laws #228-229):

> If a builder build a house for someone, and does not construct it properly, and the house which he built falls in and kills its owner, then that builder shall be put to death. If it kill the son of the owner, the son of that builder shall be put to death.

From this law, we can deduce that the son was not seen as a being separate from the father. The child was viewed as of the same substance as father. Abraham could not refuse to give what was his to God. Killing his child was therefore an appropriate punishment for the builder. This is obviously appalling to us now, but it was apparently the norm during the period of Hammurabi's code and it presumably still was the norm in Abraham's time. We can better understand the bizarre concept of human sacrifice. We can relate for a wish to give the first fruits to God. We still have this tradition for Shavuot (the Feast of Weeks). Even for humans, the Bible tells us that the male first born should be redeemed (Ex. 13:13-15), and we still do it to this day in the ceremony of the redemption of the first-born (*pidyon haben*).

In the time of Hammurabi and Abraham, the father had the right of life and death over his child, as an extension of the father's being. The child therefore could be fittingly sacrificed to the gods. In that context, when God asks Abraham to sacrifice his two first born sons (Isaac was also the first born from his mother), God is asking him to sacrifice what is part of himself; and that, Abraham could not refuse. In the same way Lot generously tried to protect the three visitors by giving away his own property, his two virgin daughters.

The Rabbis have not made it easy for us to understand this. They view Isaac as being an adult already, since, according to the Midrash quoted by Rashi, Sarah died when she learned that her son almost became a sacrifice (Rashi on Gen. 23:1). This would make Isaac about 20 years old at the time, an age at which a man was ready for the army in the days of Moses (Num. 1:2-3), and hardly a child. However the Bible uses the

118

Hebrew term *na'ar* to describe both Isaac and Ishmael (Gen. 22:5; 21:17). *Na'ar* could mean a child, a young man, or a servant. Clearly Isaac was not a servant. Abraham's reaction can be understood from an historical perspective if Isaac and Ishmael were children. In this terrifying test, Abraham is taught exactly this point in the transformation of the culture, that children are not anymore part of their father, and that they cannot be sacrificed. So, although we could say that Abraham failed the test (he should have argued with God on behalf of his sons), the lesson he learned from God's request was that ethics has changed.

Even if we can now understand Abraham's reaction, or lack of reaction, in the face of God's command, it is still difficult for us living in the 21st century (or, in the 6th millennium, if you prefer) to comprehend why Abraham, and his sons and their mothers, had to endure such a hard test by the hand of God. We could again justify it by invoking historical reason, as the Bible says: in order for everyone to know that Abraham was ready to perform a human sacrifice with his sons (Gen. 22:12 and 22:16), like the idolaters with their despicable human sacrifice. That line of historical justification works better for Abraham than for God. However our purpose here was simply to understand Abraham, not to fully comprehend an unfathomable God.

New York,
November 1st, 2020

119

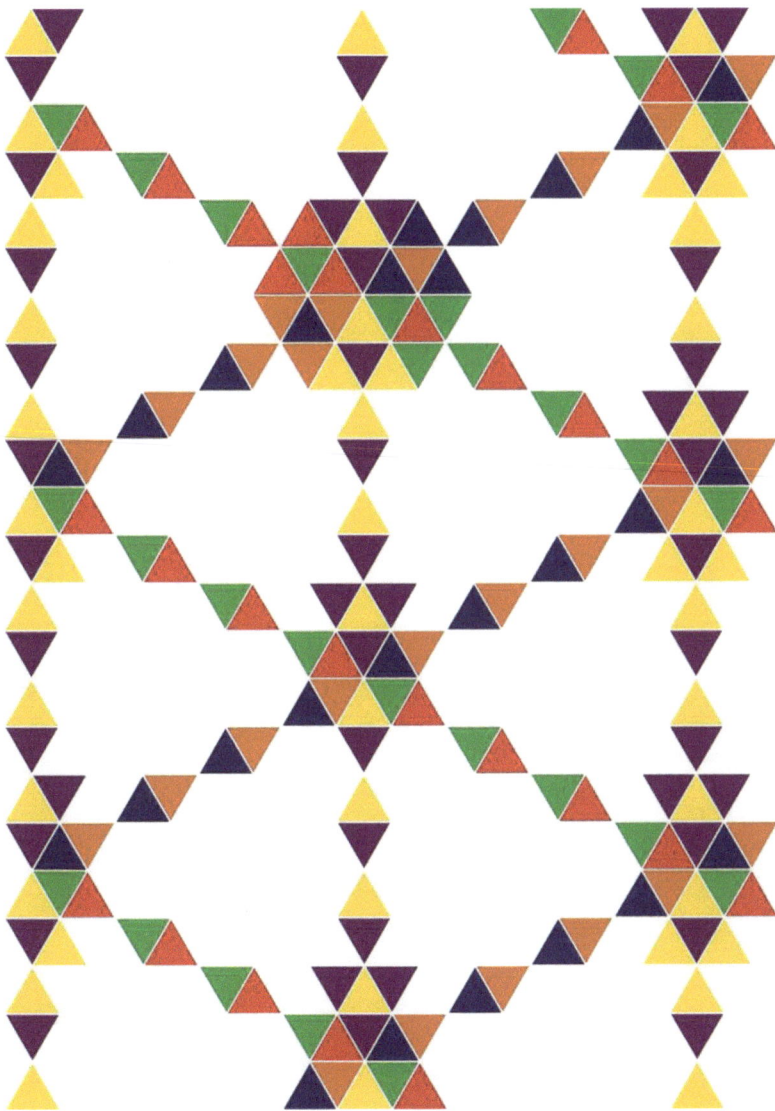

121

14 A Loud Inaudible Bang

PART ONE

The Red Sweater

I

And he cried. Not only for joy, of course, but also in sorrow. The tears were running in his heart, for he feared that one day he would hurt her, say or do something she did not like, or simply forgot that love needs nurturing lest it wither, that one day he would feel so comfortable in their relationship that he would forget her. And for this he broke the glass. Not only to remember the destruction of the temple in Jerusalem, but to remember that she, his private Jerusalem, could also be shattered by his deeds or his words, like the glass. And so he cried. May the glass cup break instead of our love, like the scapegoat, carrying our sins, sent to his death to Azazel on Yom Kippur. May his tears replace hers. And, although they were no tears on her face, he had the urge to kiss below her eyes where her tears would be, through the white veil still covering her face under the wedding canopy.

But he did not. He gazed at her precious eyes that were beaming with trust in him, looking at his tearless face, aware only of his joy and not of his sorrow. *Mazel tov*, everyone shouted. *Mazel tov*, my bride. Mazel tov, my love. Sorry if, because of your love, I ever cause you pain. Her radiant face and her hair flowing under the veil, I will remember. Even if one day I forget, I will at least remember that I should not have forgotten: hug me, kiss me. *You may now kiss the bride.* And you lifted your veil. *You silly, you think I don't know what is*

125

inside you. I know you will not break my heart, my love, you will only hurt the glass, hug me kiss me.

II

Martha was searching for the red sweater in her father's boxes. It was a unique lush piece which her mother had knitted herself. How did Diane learn to make such an amazing sweater? It looked as if it had been brought from Scandinavia, knitted with the best quality wool, thick, strong and soft at the same time. And durable. Jeffrey had worn it for 30 years and it still looked new. It was a precious gift from Diane she had made for him when they were engaged. Jeffrey would wear it sparingly, only when he went skating or skiing, while holding to the memory of the young Diane, the pretty girl in the wedding picture, laughing and full of life. Even though now Diane would not have been able to knit even a simple sweater, to him she was always the Diane of their youth, the Diane for whom he broke the glass under the wedding canopy.

In one of the boxes, Martha had found ancient pictures of the young couple. She was wearing a pretty summery, white laced cotton dress and he was wearing the red sweater, not to warm his body, but to warm his heart.

But she is the one who broke his heart. He was not the one who forgot to nurture their relationship. The sweater kept reminding him of her love, and as long as the sweater was on his heart so was her love, although in reality Diane was not capable of love anymore. She was accustomed to him and she would have been lost without him, but did she love him? *Of course silly, I still know who you are. You stand by me all those years, for better or for worse* –she would think in her moments of

126

lucidity, when the demons of Azazel gave her some respite, when she was not beating him or breaking his soul like the scapegoat on Yom Kippur. Beat him, beat him up, he is torturing you – escape, escape. And he would raise his arm – to protect himself, never to hurt her. She was not battering him; she was battering the demons of Azazel.

And he stood by her. He never broke the glass again. And he never remarried, even after she passed away. He was there not just for her, but for everyone, giving his time and attention to all who needed him. Working long hours when others would have gone home after their tour of duty, writing their note: "Attempted to reach the patient three times. Case closed. Please request new consult when the patient is interested in treatment." The other consultants would write that note and go home. But he would stay, cajoling the patients and convincing them to follow up or to go to the hospital. For this Jeffrey stayed so late that he had to rush home to take care of Diane.

Jeffrey did not divorce her, despite the abuse; because he loved her and to protect their only daughter, who would have had to leave college to come home and help take care of her mother.

Martha could not find the red sweater. But she had kept its memory, a memory of a mother who once loved, and a father who kept loving her. She, Martha, would push off suitors as unfit, comparing them to her father, or maybe to avoid the sorrow that went with the joy. And he would keep asking and pressuring her but she would ask for more time. She would not even accept a virtual kiss from him, although he thought she did when they first met virtually.

III

Last night
Magic night
From single child
To single child
From a real chimney
To a fake one with real logs
From a healer of the body
And a healer of the mind
From biker to hiker
From hiker to biker
We had virtual tea or a cup of wine
We had no dishes to make
No vacuum cleaner to pass
But we also had no hug
No goodbye kiss
To build a dream on
This is not true
Last night we had our first kisses
A first blow kiss
Virtuously virtual
And a second kiss
Virtually virtuous
Here is a third one
Kisses

IV

Martha screamed. Not just once, but twice. But did she really? The first time, yes, when she saw a mouse under her chair. She was reprimanded for being unprofessional, for being loud and emotional in the office. Her boss loved all animals, even cockroaches and she was running a tight ship.

Everyone was reprimanded routinely, twice a week on average, even Martha although her boss appreciated her greatly for her work and dedication. But there were mice and cockroaches in the building and, knowing that, Martha would avoid resting her feet on the floor under her desk.

The second time they saw a mouse in the office, her coworkers complained to the boss about it. They also took this as an opportunity to rat on Martha – maybe out of malice, or perversion, or just for the fun of bullying her, knowing she had already been reprimanded for it – by saying to their boss: "And Martha screamed!"

But Martha had not screamed, or so she claimed when she was summoned for a second time by her boss. She knew she should be in control and be composed in all situations. Maybe there was a muffled sound when she saw a mouse that second time; maybe her voice could be heard. *But she did not scream, or shout, she did not.*

Martha had an uncanny ability to tell stories about her life, detailed, vivid stories about her relations with her coworkers or with her friends. And she liked to talk. Being isolated and confined outside her working hours, they would talk on the phone almost every day, often for hours. Martha would tell him her life's stories, and he would be absorbed by her words and her laugh. He would say anything to make her laugh. It was easy. As much as Martha loved to talk, she loved to laugh, a high pitch laugh like her voice, like a little girl, a laugh he found irresistible.

Martha could also be serious when she was attacking a task even outside her work. She would push herself an extra mile when biking, or when learning something new. They read together the beginning of the Book of Lamentations during the night of Tish'a BeAv, the saddest day on the Jewish calendar, commemorating the destruction of the Temple in

Jerusalem. They would sit on the ground in the salon which was lit only by two candles, and he would teach her how to read the first verse in Hebrew. But she wanted more, she always wanted to learn more. Between her laughs, she concentrated on the shape of the new letters with their vowels marks around them, and the cantillation marks. She would ask him to repeat the verse again and again, and then she would repeat it, surprisingly well.

It was a holiday, she said, and she would not discuss this during the holiday, probably because she did not want to break his heart during that special time. But he knew already. *You can tell me* – this is not this kind of holiday, it the saddest day in the Jewish calendar a day when we are supposed to cry and mourn the loss of Jerusalem – *tell me, tell me.*

V

And so he cried. Mostly out of sorrow, of course, but also for joy. His face was tearless, and he continued to laugh with her, as the tears were running only in his heart. He took the news stoically, as if he had already known. There was no screaming, no loud emotions expressed. Just as if it had been a regular conversation. And it was, since they hardly knew each other beside those long telephone calls. She had even forbidden blowing kisses, let alone touching even her hand. But he cried nevertheless about his lost Jerusalem. He realized that he would not have the joy of mourning Jerusalem together with her by breaking a glass under a wedding canopy. But didn't they still? They had mourned Jerusalem together on that night of Tisha BeAv, and that was enough for him. Friends, we are friends she said. He couldn't take this lightly, coming from her. And because of this he had joy too.

PART TWO

Cinderella

I

She saw her petrified look reflected in his eyes. Her shoe had fallen off her right foot. She visualized him wanting to bend down, kneel, pick it up and put the shoe on her bare foot as if she were some sort of Cinderella. She heard his thoughts, they were so loud, as if he was seeing how terrified she would be if he were to play the Prince Charming. So he did not bend down or kneel.

They exchanged few words by the door, but the non-words were more important. A faint grin on his face when he gazed at her shoe. Her barely audible grumble as a response. She wanted him out now. What if he decided to stay or got loud and angry or broke things or hurt her? She didn't know him but she could hear him thinking. How strange to have in an instant such a connection with a stranger, as if their minds were two facing mirrors, reflecting each other ad infinitum. She knew that he knew that she knew what was on his mind. A perfect union, rare and complete, as if they shared a portal. She knew that he knew how scared she was, how silly she had been to announce a breakup inside her house. A breakup which was not even a breakup for her, just for him.

And then the nausea. The upsetting images shattered in a loud inaudible bang, like the exploding glass of a mirror, although no one was bodily hurt by its flying shards. What was left was nausea. She could not visualize his mind anymore, but could smell the nausea in him when they exchanged respectful words, when he reached out for the handle of the door, and when he left with a polite smile on his face, leaving shards lying on her mind, stretching the connection between them, and snapping it, ripping it apart with the whipping noise of an overextended rubber band, inflicting a sharp sting on their hands.

She closed the door and locked it behind him, although she realized that he wouldn't come back. She did not have to glance at his car parked across the street to feel that he was gone, because he too wanted to escape the nauseating smell.

Months had passed. She had almost forgotten his name. Before that, for a while, she'd dreaded his calls, even his texts. But he did not contact her. Even when the New Year came, he did not use it as an excuse to mail her a card. She wanted nothing from him. The nausea had lasted for a while, but was now gone. She had liked him initially. But no. Then there were his writings. Clever writings. Pleasant at first, but then totally misplaced and crossing the line, violating boundaries. She was so mortified that she could not even finish reading his last story. He had apologized for it several times, but it did not matter. Crossing boundaries reminded her of a dark past and she did not ever want to wander into that. She just hoped that she would never hear from him again.

And then, months later, when she had finally stopped thinking about him, she received a letter at her home. Nobody writes letters anymore, but he was different. He had put his name and address on the envelope, so she knew before opening it that it came from him. He had chosen an expensive, thick stationary for the envelope. He still knows my address, was her first thought. Nothing good could come out of that letter. She deliberated before opening it, imagined throwing it in the garbage. He knew that she did not want any reminder of him. But he had waited, patiently, many months.

132

He had shown restraint. But why was he not respecting her boundaries, again? Why was he contacting her?

The sense of nausea overpowered the nice feeling she initially experienced when remembering him. She left the letter unopened but did not throw it away. That was her first mistake. She should have thrown it out. How offensive could that letter be? Was he trying to apologize, again? She was through with him. Didn't he understand that? What was he hoping for? He knew how to write a narrative from her life story. Was it another one of his clever writings? She tried to date after him. With the pandemic it was not easy. And she was so busy at work. But there was this guy in tech who was interested in her. At least he wouldn't write distressing stories about her. He seemed dependable. They had gone on dates a few times, but she would not invite him in to her house, at least not on the second floor where her office and her bedroom were. Time. She needed time.

So, maybe she would open the letter… Maybe not. But if she ultimately had decided to carefully tear the upper part of the envelope with a knife (who had a letter opener anymore?), she would have found a three page story (another one!) starting with a neatly handwritten note:

Oh my dear, you decided to open the letter. I hope it finds you in good health and in good spirits. Below is my latest story. For your eyes only. Goodbye and be well.

Nausea

She saw in his eyes the reflection of her petrified look. Her right shoe had fallen. She visualized him wanting to bend down, kneel, pick it up and put the shoe on her bare foot as if she were some sort of Cinderella.

II

Martha read the letter-story till the end. That was her second mistake. He had pierced her with a shard of the broken mirror. What was he thinking by sending such a letter? As she was invited to by its end, she read the story again from the beginning. Was he trying to make her feel guilty? For sure he would not succeed at that. Was he trying to enter her mind again? Was the letter some kind of virus or malware destined to penetrate her brain and control it? Will there be other stories mailed to her by snail mail, or worse, as an attachment to an email, an attachment she would certainly not dare to open and risk exposing her computer to?

Even after all those months, Martha continued to use her toaster oven as her main cooking appliance. Her expensive convection oven was broken and she chose not to spend the money on a new one. She needed to save money for her son's tuition. Martha could make amazing dishes with the little toaster oven. It was the kind of challenge she was proud of, and her friends' criticisms did not touch her. A few days before the breakup—breakup for him only, since for her there was never anything to break—Stephan had bought her a simple rice cooker, to help her diversify her cooking techniques. She was still using it. The rice cooker had stopped being a reminder of how Stephan had been nice to her. That is, before the story he wrote about her.

She chopped carrots, broccoli, and sliced small tomatoes from her garden, then spread shredded cheese and herbs and salt and pepper over them before putting the dish into the toaster oven. I am not going to respond to it. It was a clever story. I hate it but I like it too. I don't want to remember the smell of nausea anymore. I have moved on. Should I send him an email telling him not to contact me anymore, or should I let it slide until he sends another story? The next one I will surely not open.

That night, Martha dreamed of her garden. She spent all her free time there. The pumpkins were growing perfectly for Halloween. In her dream, one pumpkin grew so big and so fast that she could draw a door on it with a black marker. He was there, helping her taking the weeds away. He finally had found proper gloves to protect his hands when pulling the unwanted tall stalks – leather gloves, yellow, as bright as the sun, which he kept on while they biked together down a long, twisted path that ran above a river which tumbled down a deep gorge. The path, which was dark and scarred with treacherous patches of gravel turned into a long nicely paved road through a large open urban park. On this asphalt road, they had to cut back and forth to avoid small pieces of broken glass reflecting the sun. There was more and more glass. Finally, there was so much, they had to abandon their bikes and walk instead. She could hear the sections of mirror cracking under her hiking boots. As they walked, the pieces got bigger and bigger, their multiple facets throwing the sun in angles at their eyes. She realized it was a huge broken mirror, or maybe two. Using big data and machine learning, a computer could see the puzzle and put the pieces back together. She sat down and tried to program the software, alone at first, but it was beyond her ability. She enlisted the help of her uncle, her father's brother, a computer wizard, expert in machine learning, and she finally created the right program. When she pressed ENTER, the computer started to think and the glass pieces vibrated, as if they wanted to move. Time, she needed time. The clock was ticking. Oh no, in her rush, her right shoe had fallen, and she only had a slipper on her left foot. Where was her right glass slipper? She looked at him, bending to reach something on the floor. Had he found it? Would he take her ankle and delicately slip her bare foot into the glass shoe? No, time was running out. *Gong.* Another gong. She noticed a huge yellow pumpkin, its door drawn by a black magic marker, standing next to her. The door opened. The gongs were now replaced by the buzzing sound of an alarm clock. *Bip. Bip.* She needed more time. Quickly, she reached for the snooze button, but the brusque movement of her hand turned her, and shifted her foot, which pushed the glass shoe to the ground. It shattered, mixing its shards with the broken mirrors. The computer had finished its analysis and the broken pieces of the mirrors rose straight up, then twirled like the twister in movies like the Wizard of Oz, and formed two large standing mirrors. But the shattered glass of her broken shoe had interfered with the computer analysis, and the mirrors were not perfectly aligned as each other's images. She tried to enter the portal formed by their endless reflections, but the defects prevented her from moving and reaching the other side. So she stood there. He had disappeared but she saw the refection of his image trapped inside the mirror. His lips were moving but she could not hear his voice. Maybe he was trying to contact her? She could no longer read his mind. Maybe he would text, or send a letter? Maybe. But she did not want any of this anymore. All this twirling adventure had made her dizzy, and when she woke up, she had a nauseating taste in her mouth.

New York,
November 4, 2020

136

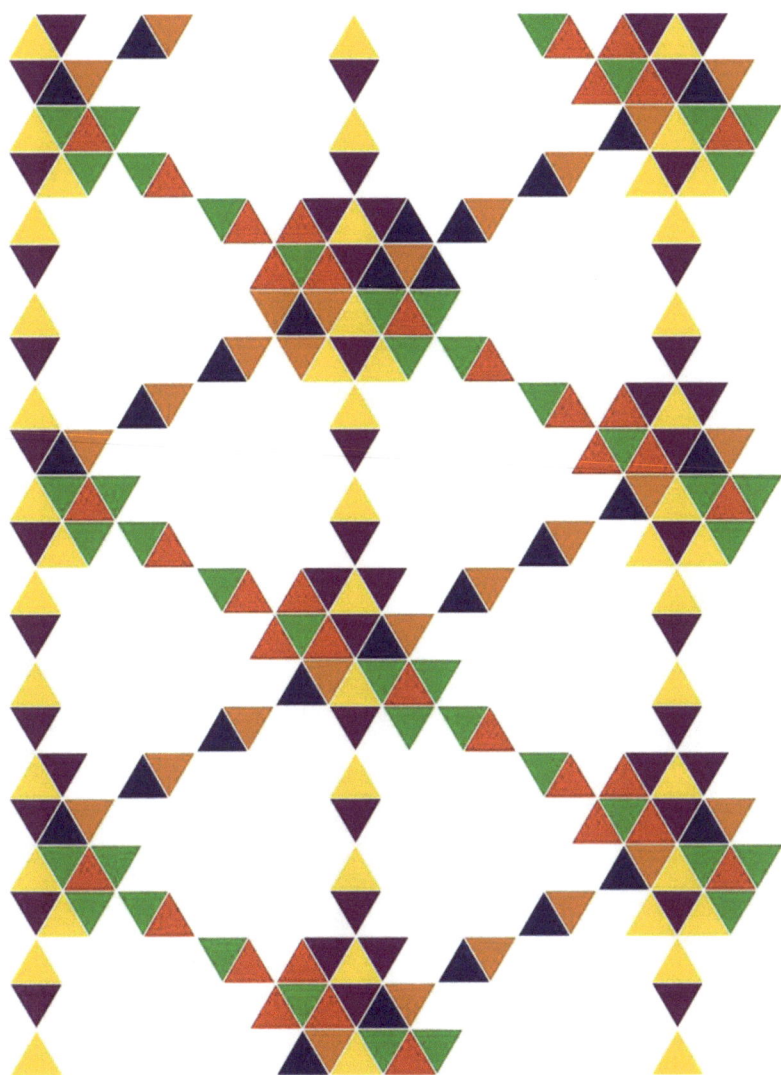

15 Maya

You should have someone take you home, said Laurie: Can I go with you? Maya supported this counsel with a concerned nod, and they – Laurie and Maya – both waited for her response. Laurie, tall, sure of herself, with striking, long blond hair, was driven and competitive and more forceful with her advice. Maya, as usual for her, was softer and more discreet.

The obvious answer was Yes. Maybe if Maya had been the only one asking... But Ariel felt that she was a big girl and did not need a chaperon to take a cab home that night, even in her current outfit. Laurie had introduced Ariel, her friend, to a crowd Maya and she belonged to. Ariel had never talked privately with Maya, and Maya had never approached Ariel or tried to send her any signals; although the two met regularly at a potluck dinner that was held, often as much as once a week, at the house or apartment of one of the group's members. Everyone in this group would also occasionally all go out together to the theater or a restaurant. But today was different; they had attended a dress-up party. Ariel had asked around if she could borrow a wig. And Maya gave her one as a gift. A neat blond wig, with hair going down a little lower than Ariel's ears. Ariel should have taken the gift of the wig as clue of Maya's interest. And then, after Ariel and Laurie got to the party, and Ariel sat on the faux leather couch, Maya burst out impulsively with admiration and envy: Oh, you have nice legs! Did you shave? That also should have been a clue. But Ariel was blinded by the pride she took from Maya's compliment, and concentrated only on how to carefully answer the question, without noticing Maya's feelings. Ariel was known to have quite hairy legs which she would never shave or cover with pantyhose, as if to say that she did not care what the boys would think of her. As if saying: this is how she was, and there was no reason to change. Either you like me or you don't, this is who I am. No, Ariel had not shaved. She had a little secret which she was embarrassed to reveal. Ariel had put on two pairs of pantyhose, one on top of the other: a skin-colored pantyhose, to mask her hairy legs, and a sheer black one over that, for the look. Ariel, the nerdy girl with glasses, often wearing pants, did dress up tonight. And Maya, who was as reserved as Ariel—Ariel should definitely have taken that clue—mumbled almost to herself (commenting again on Ariel's look), I feel naked, like you now know all my intimate secrets. Maya would never have gone out bare-legged, and she did not usually wear pants like Ariel.

The thought of Maya never entered Ariel's mind. Or if it did, it was immediately pushed back as impossible because Ariel could not betray her friendship with Laurie. Laurie would have been not just jealous – Laurie was the jealous and possessive type – , she would have been humiliated in her circle of friends, a nice group of single girls and boys, all in their 20's, or thereabouts.

Before arriving at the dress-up party, Ariel had gone to Laurie's to get a thorough makeover. Laurie was standing with her long, lush golden hair shining over Ariel's face, neck and breast. Laurie's hair brushed over her when she bent to reach the seat where Ariel's eyes, cheeks and lips were blossoming from the collar of a thin black dress. Laurie visibly took pleasure applying the foundation, using different light brushes to makeup Ariel's impassive face and eyebrows, underlining the eyes and the lips, rubbing the eyelids in circles with a beige powder above the eyeliner. Before the final touch, the cherry lipstick she had chosen for Ariel, Laurie, tantalized by her own creation, slightly lifted Ariel's collar to have a peak at her bosom, and tried to kiss Ariel, strongly, forcefully, unexpectedly. But Ariel resisted, like she resisted later that night, as the inexperienced girl she was, closing her thighs together, when that boy at the party, with his three-day-old black beard – she did not even know his name –, sat next to her on the couch facing Maya. He tried to lift her pleated dress, not only with his lusty hands but also with his eyes, big round dilated eyes, oozing with desire. Ariel had never before felt such a gaze directed at her, and it scared her, although she felt safe at the party with Maya and Laurie nearby, and although later on, years after the party was over, Ariel took pleasure reimagining that look aimed at her, as a young attractive woman.

It was different from the furtive looks Ariel noticed, a few years later, with Sasha, her former lover, after they met at a party at someone's house. Ariel had moved on, but she still had felling for Sasha and Ariel almost cried when they met privately in a bedroom away from the noise of the party. Later in that house, while Sasha's boyfriend was in another room, Sasha sat on the floor of the hallway with her skirt rolled up, and she caught the gaze of an older boy staring at her legs. Ariel noticed that Sasha looked at the older boy intensely with a smile acknowledging his interest, without attempting to cover her legs spread out on the floor. The boy, who knew the boyfriend and knew of Sasha's past with Ariel, looked straight back at Sasha. Ariel saw what was in his look, a mixture of astonishment and reproach for Sasha's brazen attitude. She was a tease who enjoyed stirring up attention. Sasha lowered her eyes first. Ariel realized that it had been for the best that Sasha and she were no longer together.

Ariel should have listened to them. Although she could not have asked Maya to accompany her home instead of Laurie, Ariel could have asked the two friends to both go with her. Instead, Ariel went home alone to her studio on the third floor of a dingy walkup building. And on the way up, here he was, drunk, the neighbor, offended or excited by her look, or both, coming up the steep and narrow staircase not far behind her. He was loud, staggering, threatening. Ariel, unsteady in her high heeled shoes, but still faster than he was, quickly made it into her apartment and locked her door before the drunk caught up to her, just in time.

Ariel never returned the wig to Maya, and Laurie never crossed boundaries again with Ariel. Ultimately, Ariel left the group, without Maya or Ariel ever having asked each other out, because of their misplaced fear of betraying Laurie. And Ariel wondered, years after the dress-up party, if things could have ended, or rather started, differently.

New York
November 8, 2020

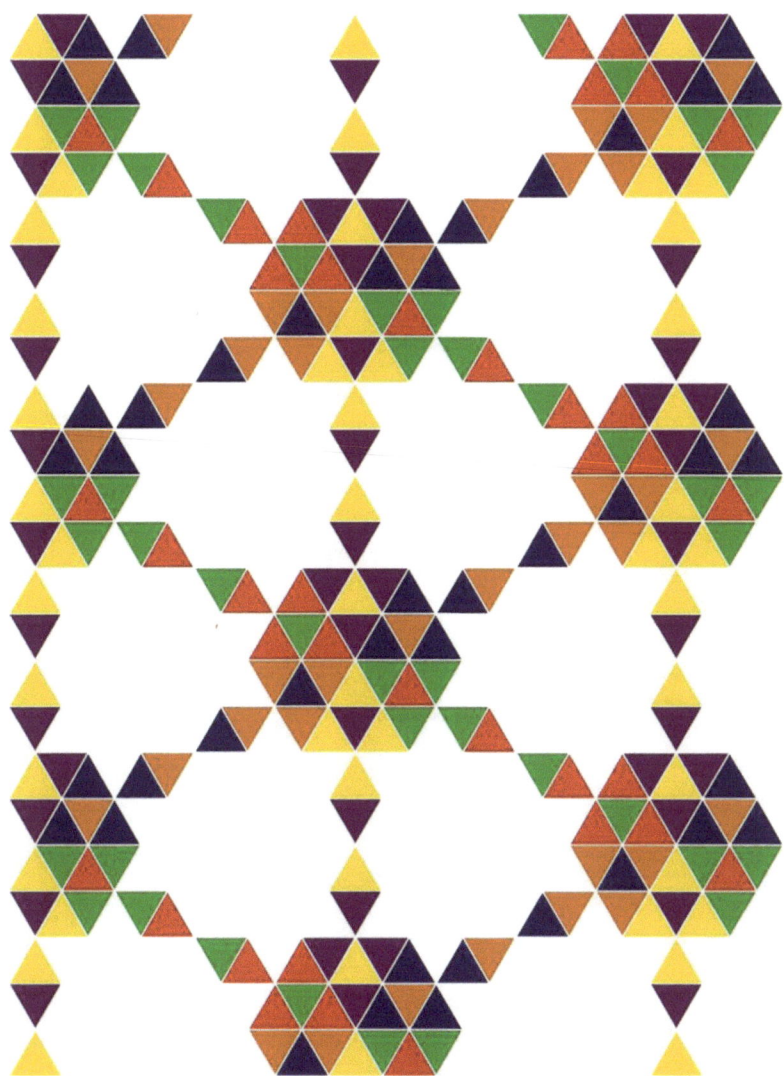

16 The Blessing of the Hands

He had to explain *samakh,* the Hebrew term, to Nadia, so she could understand what the Blessing of the Hands meant to him. For her it was a "secular" blessing, where she would bless the hands of a coworker and through them the work he was doing, a work done with hands entering formulas on a keyboard, repairing systems that had crashed, or programing sophisticated communications networks.

Nadia had innocent deep blue-green eyes, a broad and genuine smile, and a disarming faith in the goodness of all God's creatures. She always wore a modest pale blue or light beige, long-pleated dress. She was the pastor's daughter. But she had gotten a degree in computer science rather than religion like her father, who supported and adored her. She enjoyed math and information technology, and was good at these. In the office, it did not trouble her that she was the only woman in the I.T. department. She looked people in the eyes, naturally, without ulterior motives, with something like a child's openness, or maybe as Eve would have in the Garden of Eden. The young single men in the I.T. department did not dare to flirt with her. They felt that Nadia was too far out of their reach, somewhere in the neighborhood of the angels.

He had missed the day when Nadia performed the blessings with all her colleagues in the I.T. department, so she offered to perform the ritual with him separately. Everyone, religious or not, believer or atheist, single men or married with kids, had agreed to receive her "secular" blessing and words of comfort, after the first scare of the pandemic. For this private service, she would have to bring her oil to rub on his hands to bless them. He could not remember the last time a stranger had even touched his hands, let alone rubbed oil on them, in this time of Corona. Rub it in circles, had she said? Would she hold his hands in her left hand, and with her right hand apply the oil (would it be pure olive oil, scented with myrrh?), stir it on his palm or on the back of his hands; and then give him her blessing with an invisible smile through her mask, with her soft, gentle voice? She was naïve if she thought that she would only be stirring the oil, and that this was merely a secular blessing. She would be stirring heaven and earth, pastor's daughter that she was. He did not believe in the secular nature of her blessing, and he was fine with that. Secular was not his thing anyway. For him it had the vibes of a religious ceremony. Anointed? He thought of the anointing of the High Priest, the King, the King Messiah/the anointed one/the *mashiach*, with the anointing oil, the *shemen ha-mishchah*, smeared—rubbed?—on their head.

> **The Sages taught: How does one anoint the kings?** One smears the oil in a manner that is **similar to** the form of **a crown** around his head. **And** how does one anoint **the priests?** One smears the oil in a shape **like** the Greek letter **chi (X).** The Gemara (Talmud) asks: **What** is the meaning of: **Like the Greek letter chi? Rav Menashya bar Gadda said:** [Pronounced] **Like the Greek** equivalent of the Hebrew letter **kaf.** (Talmud Horayot 12a)[22]

Would she rub the oil in a circle on his hand, or would she make a cross like the shape of the Greek letter chi? Would she touch his palms or the back his hands?

He was wrong. She did not hold his hands. She did not rub them or even touch them. She asked him to join his hands facing upward, and from above she poured a few drops of frankincense essential oil on his palms. She had given him a

---

[22] According to Rav Menashya bar Gadda, (circa 320 C.E.–350 C.E), quoted in this passage from the Babylonian Talmud, the Greek letter chi (X or χ) was pronounced at that time like the Hebrew letter kaf (כ), as in Ancient Greek; or like the letter khaf (כ), as in Modern Greek.

English translation from Hebrew adapted from www.sefaria.org.

146

choice between frankincense and lavender. He chose the ancient spice because of its biblical connotations. It reminded him of the holy oil perfumed with frankincense, used in the Divine service in the Tabernacle.

> And the LORD said unto Moses, Take unto thee sweet spices, stacte, and onycha, and galbanum; these sweet spices with pure frankincense: of each shall there be a like weight: And thou shalt make it a perfume, a confection after the art of the apothecary, tempered together, pure and holy: And thou shalt beat some of it very small, and put of it before the testimony in the tabernacle of the congregation, where I will meet with thee: it shall be unto you most holy. (Ex. 30:34-36)[23]

But mostly, he thought of the Song of Songs, an allegory for the mutual yearning between God and mankind.

> Thy plants are an orchard of pomegranates, with pleasant fruits; camphire, with spikenard, spikenard and saffron; calamus and cinnamon, with all trees of frankincense; myrrh and aloes, with all the chief spices: A fountain of gardens, a well of living waters, and streams from Lebanon. Awake, O north wind; and come, thou south; blow upon my garden, that the spices thereof may flow out. Let my beloved come into his garden, and eat his pleasant fruits. (Song of Sg. 4:13-16)

Now rub your hands, she said. And he did. And she instructed him again to put his palms up side by side, and she placed her own hands facing down, her palms hovering above his, at a respectful and safe distance, but close nevertheless, and she looked him in the eyes, her grey blue-green eyes, peaking out above a surgical mask covering her nose, her cheeks, and lips, and she pronounced her blessing like an oracle, improvising, based on a formula written on a simple sheet of paper she had placed over the large finely wrought golden cross on the cover of her Bible. She blessed not only

---

[23] All Biblical quotations in this chapter follow the King James Version.

the hands but the spirit guiding them. She kept up her gaze, looking into his eyes, and flooded him with her inspired blessing: from her eyes to his eyes, from her hands to his hands.

Blessed be these hands that have felt love and death.
Blessed be these hands that have embraced others with compassion.
Blessed be these hands that have held pain, faced fears, and offered comfort.

May you be blessed with a spirit of strength and kindness.
May you be blessed with a spirit of compassion for others and for yourself.

May your work help others and yourself through your hands.
So, Blessed be your hands for they are a conduit of the love you hold in your heart.

Without being prompted, he responded amen to her blessings, just as at the end of a religious ceremony.

She thought the moment had passed and was over. But as she was turning away to leave, he asked her if he could give her, in return, his own blessing with his now blessed hands. For him, the expression "blessing of the hands" was a translation from the Hebrew, and he associated it with all the meanings of the Hebrew word *samakh*. The blessing of the hands was the "imposition of the hands," the laying on of the hands during the priestly blessing. *Samakh* did not mean his hands below facing upward receiving the blessing, but her hands above facing downwards giving the blessing. She listened to his description of the different meanings of the Hebrew verb *samakh* (סמך), along with some Bible quotes:

Support; Sustain
Lay upon (hands)
Bring near; Move closer together
Lean (physically)
Rely on; Depend; Trust

148

Authorize; Ordain (rabbis, teachers)

Support: The LORD **upholdeth** all that fall, and raiseth up all those that be bowed down. (Ps. 145:14)

Lay upon: And he shall **put** his hand **upon** the head of the burnt offering; and it shall be accepted for him to make atonement for him. (Lev. 1:4)

Move closer together: He did not give a biblical quote, but he related the verb *samakh* to another Hebrew verb *qarav* (קרב). He explained that the root those two verbs means "to draw close," and are they are both related to offering a sacrifice. The Hebrew word for sacrifice (*qorban*) comes from the same root of the verb *qarav*. When we bring a *qorban*, an offering, it draws God closer to us.[24] When we lay the hands on the head of a sacrifice, or on the head of someone being blessed or of a rabbi being ordained, we also draw a close connection with them. And not only with them, but with the ancestors who passed on that ritual to us, and their ancestors too, connecting all the way back and up to the Divine source.

He extended his hands over her head, without touching her hair. Then he began with words he improvised for her:

> May all the hands you blessed be a source of blessing for you.
> May those hands be a testimony to the comfort you provided to others.
> May they comfort you in return.
> May you continue to be a source of blessing for all around you.

Then he recited the priestly blessing:

> The Lord bless thee, and keep thee:
> The Lord make his face shine upon thee, and be gracious unto thee:

---

[24] See: Sefer HaBahir (section 109).

The Lord lift up his countenance upon thee, and give thee peace.[25]

He had first recited the priestly blessing in Hebrew, strange fascinating words she did not comprehend, except the last one, "Shalom" (peace). She closed her eyes to absorb the gift of the blessing and kept them closed when he repeated it in English. It was an interior moment for her, a connection to the Divine through the medium of the ancient words. She did not see the surprise, mixed with some embarrassment, in his eyes when she closed hers. He was wondering if he should also have closed his, earlier during her blessing. She was listening carefully to the benediction being bestowed upon her, and she accepted it with gratitude and humility.

Amen, she said, opening her eyes to unmask some of her soul above the mask she was wearing. She thanked him, and then in silence she turned her slight frame away and left, thinking of the interior blessed moment she had just experienced. She had come to give a secular blessing to others, and she left having been given a Divine blessing.

New York
November 26, 2020

---

[25] Num. 6: 24-26

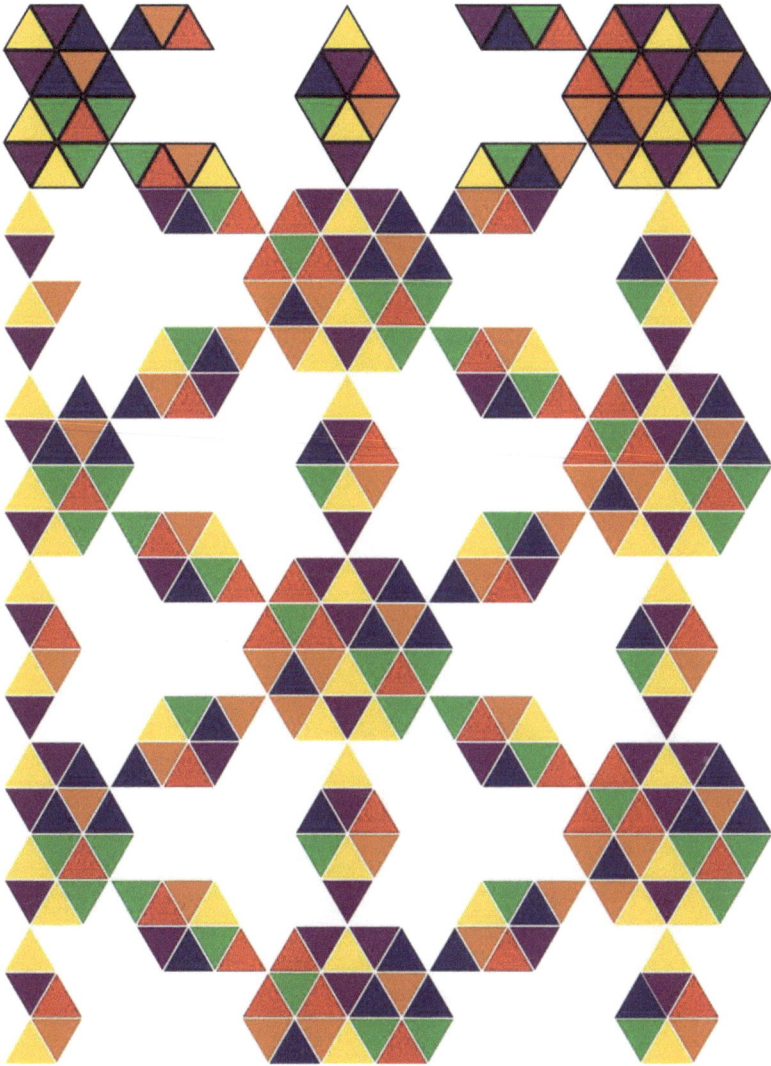

17 Stone-Words

Love. Of course he did not mention it. Of course she did not hear it. It was buried in heaven within acceptable and proper language about connecting with God. But here and there, hints surfaced briefly and surprisingly from the text, shiny stone-words bringing down earthly love, unmasked – only for this love to be pushed back up toward high spiritual clouds, covered by lofty-words. He had been careful in his language not to say anything offensive or harassing. But the words were there in the scriptures, double entendres expressing both the spiritual love between God and mankind and the physical one between men and women. The same words could be seen as spiritual lofty-words or earthly stone-words. He covered his tracks by explaining it as spiritual allegory, the heavenly, over the earthly yearning. She felt called to be a spiritual teacher, but not in Judaism. Her spirituality attracted him; however she was not into romantic love, or so he gathered, or so she tried to project, all wrapped in her own personal path of spirituality. Maybe that was also her cover, like his lofty words were for him.

When he chanted:

> I would lead you, I would bring you to the house of my mother, of her who taught me— I would let you drink of the spiced wine, of my pomegranate juice.
> Your cheeks behind your veil: like a pomegranate split open.[26]

He could have, at least, first quoted Rashi's medieval commentary:

---

[26] Song of Songs 8:2 and 4:3. Modified JPS translation

153

Your cheeks: This is the upper part of the face, called *pomels* in [old] French, next to the eyes.[27] And in the language of the Talmud, it is called "the pomegranate of the face." It resembles the split half of a pomegranate from the outside, which is red and round, praise for a woman's beauty.

And then he would have recited a poem he had composed for her:

> Invisible behind the veil
> Your rosy cheeks
> Your crimson lips
> Out of reach out of touch
> Out of taste out of kiss
> Oozing of fragrant red wine
> Dripping of pomegranate juice
>
> Impossible yearning
> Forbidden passion

But he did not.

He did not praise the pomegranate seeds as red, shiny stone-words of human love. Instead, he used pomegranates as lofty-words, symbolizing God's holy words of Torah, His holy commandments, His love for His female companion, for His people, and for His human creation:

> One who sees **slices of pomegranates** in his dream, **if he is a Torah scholar, he should anticipate Torah, as it is stated: "I would let you drink of the spiced wine, of my pomegranate juice"** (Song of Songs 8:2), which is traditionally understood as an allusion to Torah. **And if** the dreamer **is an ignoramus, he should anticipate mitzvot (Divine commandments),** as it is stated: **"Your cheeks are like a split pomegranate"** (Song of Songs 4:3). As the Talmud was previously interpreted homiletically: **What is** the meaning of the word **"Your cheeks**

---

[27] In modern French: *Pommette* (cheekbone)

[*rakatekh*]"? **Even the most ignorant [*reikanin*] among you,** Israel, **are full of mitzvot like a pomegranate.**[28]

Instead he talked about Jacob's stones representing his connection with the Divine.

> The stones fought
> To be the one under Jacob's head
> Me, me, me
> So He united them
> And they were one
>
> With his head on that stone
> His spirit went up on the ladder
> Two angels went up
> Two angels went down[29]

But then he uncovered himself by also talking about another of Jacob's stones, this one connecting Jacob to Rachel, his true love.

> One big stone
> Covering the well
> Too large to be moved
> By one shepherd alone
>
> Jacob moved the stone
> Alone, all by himself
> To show Rachel his passion
> And free the flow of water
> From the well.

---

[28] Babylonian Talmud, Berakhot: 57a. In Hebrew, only the consonants are written. The Talmud plays with the word RKTKh (רקתך). Instead of reading RaKaTeKh (your cheeks), with the traditional vocalization of the Masoretic text, the Talmud empties the text of its physical and sensual meaning, and reads ReiKaTeKh (your empty/ריקתך) from ReiK (empty/ריק/רק). The Talmud interprets "your empty" as meaning "your people empty of the knowledge in Torah," meaning, your most ignorant people (Translation modified from The William Davidson Talmud).
[29] See Genesis 28:11-12 with Rashi's commentary.

155

However, realizing he may have committed an indiscretion, he tried to cover his tracks. He talked about the kabbalah, and how the flux of water was a symbol of desired union between the Jacob, representing the masculine aspect of the Divine— the emanation of Beauty called the *sefira Tiferet*—and the Rachel, representing the feminine aspect of the Divine, the Divine Presence. Nevertheless, even that esoteric imagery was still too erotic, too explicit, so he further covered it up by talking about meditation techniques.

But he was wrong again. She, of all people, so wrapped up with her years of solitary meditation, responded to him, with surprising words, not tender words yet, but opening words:

And I must confess that our talk awakened the romantic in me…

Although she closed them again, elusive, putting a veil over her precious-stone-words, covering her nose, her cheeks, and her lips:

Although it is not all that wonderful at all!

New York
November 27, 2020

18 Verbal Jousting

Excited, almost jittery, with fresh, new thoughts burgeoning and bursting into her mind, only to be damped down or nipped in the bud by an extreme tiredness, the result of sleep deprivation mixed with a caffeine overdose, Chaya tried to stay in control. Like an overmedicated, manic woman, she tried to resist abandoning the field of an already lost battle, not ready yet to tip over her king and give up at this chess match of her mind against herself. Control. She had to stay in control. And she had lost it when he had shut down his profile, obscuring not only his image, but more importantly his words and HER words. What right did he have? Stranger. He is a stranger to me. It does not matter; but it did. She needed to reflect back on his original words, and review her own, her own words, which she would always stich and weigh cautiously. Words. She was in love with words. Certainly not with him. But with his words, maybe there was an appreciation, although the critic in her had uncovered many flaws in his stories. Had she used the word "stilted" to describe one of his writing? *Elle ne mâchait pas ses mots*, she did not mince her words, and would dispense precise and acerbic commentaries when deserved, which gave more weight to the praise she did confer. But really, she was neither chewing on nor mincing her words. Words were her life, carefully chosen precious words, which she tasted slowly in her mouth like a *bloc de foie gras* or a thick piece of salmon sashimi, dissolving their complex flavor and fragrance.

He imagined her sitting at home, at her desk in front of her computer, in a comfortable office chair wearing that black leather skirt he had seen her in, though, most likely, she would be writing in sweatpants or even pajama pants, something more comfortable, while still wearing a professional and sober top, probably also black, with a touch

159

of jewelry, to project a conservative-but-still-somewhat-funky image on her zoom conferences with her editor and the other staff of her web based journal.

"Funny how we critique each other's stories." He started typing from his opulent, brown leather armchair which he had chosen as a reminder of a cozy reading room in the Butler Library at Columbia University, his laptop niched on a pillow over his thighs. The wall of his study was obscured by a tapestry of books illuminating the room from the floor to the ten-foot-high ceiling with their brilliant insights piercing from a world of darkness.

"In the story of *Mindy* I sent you earlier, you criticized rightly the lack of substance of the characters, and you wondered how relevant the lesbian context was. You encouraged me to emphasize the disguise and the concealment aspects in the story. And even after the last revision, when Arielle, the main protagonist was now concealed (or revealed?) as a man who for a few hours that day was taking the role of a woman, you glossed over Arielle's feelings. Three times that day she experienced not only an unfulfilled yearning for Mindy, but also actual sexual harassment. The first time when the heroine's girlfriend, while giving her a makeover, forcefully kissed her against her will, and then when that boy at the party lifted her skirt (while she was still in the safety of Mindy watching over her); and finally when she came home alone and encountered a scary drunk neighbor from whom she barely escaped despite the handicap of fleeing in her high heel shoes. Maybe you actually answered or at least related to that story even if you didn't seem to appreciate it, when you sent me, afterwards, your new story of a woman raped by her date, a disturbing story written with some distance and humor.

And I too commented on your style, and not on the content, and I revised your text to make it even more

160

disturbing. Not a word or question from me or from you, about the source of our stories or the emotions attached to them. As if our preoccupation with the form and style was intellectual masturbation which could deflect the blow of the described abuse. What a bizarre bunch of literary critics we are!"

He paused before sending her his comments on their previous exchanges. His back slid down along the soft lumbar cushions of his deep library armchair and his feet extended far out along the large pouf (she would probably prefer calling it an ottoman—Were the Turks involved in this piece of furniture like the turkey of Thanksgiving?). His thoughts were derailed and he fell into a half sleep instead of pressing SEND, then... accidentally erased his comments, which he had foolishly not saved. And so she never received this critique, and they continued safely in their exchange, their intellectual *joute oratoire* (verbal jousting), avoiding the risk of venturing too deeply into the dark places of their personal histories.

New York
January 10, 2021

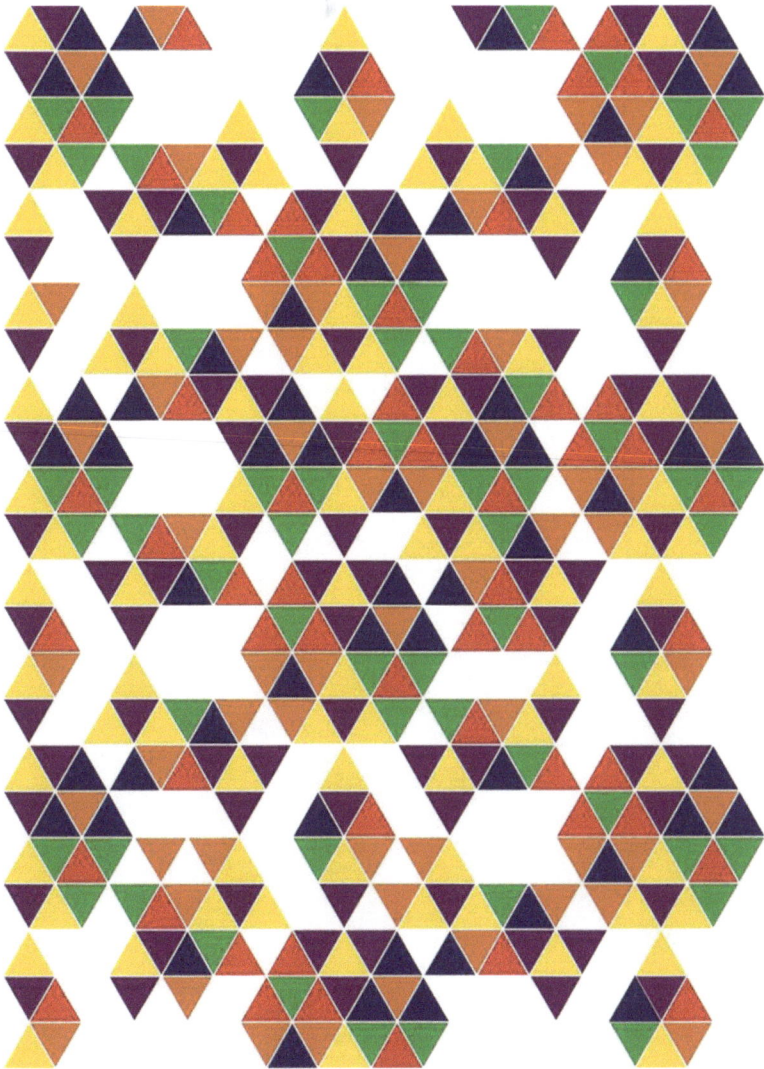

19 A Thousand Camels for Your Gazelle

I

Layla woke up at 3 a.m. that night with hunger in her oversized belly. Naked, she rose from her cherry tree blossom sheets, walking toward the kitchen, through a dark hallway, to her unlit dining room. In the dining room there was enough light for her to fumble around the familiar surroundings, but not enough for her neighbors across the tiny courtyard to get a peek of her walking undressed. For a moment she thought of siting on her *zafu*, a black meditation cushion, but instead she retreated to her bedroom, turned up the electric dial of a small oil radiator and slid back in between her empty sheets.

Was it too early for her to get rid of her wedding dress? Layla's thoughts stumbled indecisively, just as she had moments before wandered through her empty house. Would it bring the evil eye? Was it a bad omen to keep the dress she had bought three months ago? It was still in its original long shiny white box, sitting on the floor by the other side of her queen-size bed, an untouched relic of a more hopeful time. Layla turned off the lamp on her overstuffed nightstand and tried to return to her dream.

And she fell back into the *shook* of the old city, still crowded with tourists as before. *Mille chameaux pour ta gazelle!* "A thousand camels for your gazelle!" A playful call from a middle-aged Arab shopkeeper merged from a souk of another continent. She had learned to use the Arabic pronunciation *souk* for the same kind of market as the *shook* of the old city.

A thousand camels! An exorbitant price for a dowry when the worth of a young woman was still counted in camels, in a language where beauty (جمال/jamal) had the same root letters as camel (جمل/jamal). How many buckets of water would she need to lift from the well to satisfy a thirsty stranger, in search of a bride for his master, who asked for water at the end of his long journey? גם לגמליך אשאב עד אם־כלו לשתת *(Gam ligmaleykha esh'av ad im-kilu lishtot)* "I will draw water for you and also for your camels, until they finish drinking," was her response, like Rebecca. If a thirsty camel after a long trek in the desert can drink 100 litters of water, 1000 camels would drink...

She passed the shops sparkling with cheap brass jewelry, and finally reached the Armenian pottery shop. There, in the Jerusalem *shook*, the hand-crafted blue designs were even more striking than their Moroccan counterparts in the souk of Marrakesh. And she found it, a large slightly conic, flowery blue and white plate which would hold a generous measure of the family's traditional couscous rising like a mountain and dotted with delicious meat and vegetables. At the center of the plate was an empty white dot inside a simple blue circle that would serve well as the focus point of a Mandala for meditation. Layla never thought of focusing on that point when she sat on her *zafu*, because the plate was hung too high in the wall of her apartment in Paris.

The deep plate had been brought back painstakingly years before from that same shop in Jerusalem by her father, in a large piece of carry-on luggage carefully placed under the seat on the plane to Paris. But the plate had fallen from the wall, pushed by a *jinn* (genie), or by *mazikin*, malefic spirits emboldened by the evil eye. To ward off the bad omen, her father shouted joyfully "Mazel tov!" attempting to convert this broken piece of Jerusalem into a good charm, like the broken glass would have been at her wedding.

When she woke up in her sheets decorated with Japanese cherry tree blossoms, Layla did not recognize the blossoms as the good luck symbol newlywed Japanese couples flock under to take their wedding pictures. The broken Armenian plate had been swept up from her living room floor a long time ago, and thrown away rather than being preserved as some couples preserve their broken wedding glass. The long white box lying on the floor was already hidden from the view, but Layla pushed it with her foot further under the bed.

II

Layla entered the narrow open path between pottery of different sizes piled up on the floor in front of shelves and covering the walls, floor to ceiling, with the largest most striking and more expensive pieces hung high in the Armenian pottery shop in the *shook*. The shop was more modest and homey than the large fancy boutique with its original designs signed by contemporary Armenian artists on Shlomzion Hamalka Street, down the infamous Jerusalem *Misrad hapenim* (ministry of interior). Her father entered first, and the old shop owner greeted him with genuine pleasure: مرحبا ابو ليلى! *(marhaba Abu Layla!)* "Hello, Father of Layla!" And, looking only at him while acknowledging his already grown daughter, the shopkeeper repeated the ancient pleasantry to her father with a smile of playful connivance and appreciation. ألف جمال لغزالك! *('alf jemal lighazalak!)* "A thousand camels for your gazelle!"

The identical large ceramic couscous plate was hanging there at the same spot it had been kept before, when she had accompanied her father to buy the original plate in his favorite shop. The empty eye in its center radiated graciously from the top of the left wall in the back of the shop, the most secure place of the *magasin*/مخزن (makhzin)/מחסן (makhsan) /(shop). When Layla, who was now more than just a grown daughter, looked at the shopkeeper, her father and the old owner had disappeared. The shopkeeper was replaced by his son who resembled the shopkeeper in the local grocery by her grandmother's office in Paris. When her father went once with his older daughter to retrace his steps in the old neighborhood of his mother, he had found the grocery still standing. The old shopkeeper remembered the grandmother very well, and confirmed that when she first opened her practice across the street when he was still a youthful man, he had brought her as a welcome gift a package of beautiful dates, a traditional present among people of the desert for thousands of years. When her father returned to the shop a year later with his younger daughter, the shopkeeper's son who did not know Layla's grandmother, had taken over and informed them that the old man had stayed *au pays*, in the old country most likely Algeria. However, even if the old man and the grandmother were no longer there, the story had been preserved, along with the act of kindness of the Arab shopkeeper to a woman stranger.

Speaking now in Hebrew instead of English, not wanting to be taken for a foreign tourist who did not know how to bargain, Layla enquired about the large plate. She pretended to have just noticed it, hiding her enthusiasm, acting as if the plate had no pressing importance for her, though she knew that there was no way she would leave the shop without that plate.

168

III

Why?

Why had her heart caught fire, once more, after so long? Why had she fallen for his soft eyes, his mild manners, his timid smile, his broken feelings? Why did she feel comfortable so soon to walk the shadow of her fingers, slowly, delicately, down the shadow of his face on the wall that evening, with her shadow barely brushing his? Why did he let her hair caress his shoulder once, inadvertently? Why was his heart moved at their contact, his smile brightened. Why did his eyes widen? Why did he promise to care for her and comfort her? Why did he make plans to be happy with her, to forget his sorrow and hers? Why did he call her that day, as unexpectedly as a hot spring day in the middle of a bitter winter, to make his announcement? Why did he sound so scared on the phone? Why did he refuse to meet face to face despite her pleading, begging for just one more time?

One more time I wanted to meet
For you to tell me face to face
Why you changed your heat
Into ice
Why you broke your promises
Into pieces

To understand why
To say goodbye
To give a last chance
To a stillborn romance
To be combative
To forgive
To close
To be close
One more time

The next night, Layla woke up hungry again, as if someone was devouring her stomach from the inside. Instead of appeasing her hunger by opening the fridge, she decided to dwell on that internal sensation and observe it from the outside as a curiosity not belonging to her. The feeling of hunger was to be seen as something precious to look into. Maybe she would sit on her *zafu* and concentrate on that feeling of hunger, imagining the absurd scenario of starving in an apartment that was stocked for a siege. She would be waiting for the hunger to come, expecting it like a distant friend who would rarely visit for more than a few minutes at a time. She knew that she would have to fight with her ancestors who had suffered real hunger and starvation, and she would argue that by eating now she wouldn't be able to save them. That her ancestors' fear of hunger belonged to another era, not applicable to her, here and now. And she knew that she would likely lose the fight that night and that she would try again the night after. Failing again and again, until her belly grew and in the pangs of labor she gave birth not to the messiah but to a malefic genie, under the same spell which Rachel had endured when just after giving birth with her last breath she named her baby "Ben-Oni" ("the son of my sorrow"). Her husband Jacob straightaway changed his son's name to "Benjamin" ("the son of my right hand" or "son of my old age") to undo the evil spell which he, Jacob, had unknowingly put on Rachel, by cursing whoever stole the idol. Because of Jacob's curse Layla suffered hunger, or rather she suffered not being able stand hunger and stop eating during this time of loss, when her hope had been smashed and she was sleeping on a bed atop this smashed hope neatly folded in a long shiny box. But then she would remember that three years ago, seven years after her divorce, she had the courage to throw away that bag she had kept all those years containing the glass broken at her wedding. She had never opened the white cloth bag, to avoid getting pricked by the shards, but she would at times take it and shake it a bit to hear the pieces clanging and singing, reassuring her that they were still inside. For a while she had some regrets about letting go of that white bag, but not anymore. She would meet someone who would make her laugh again, with whom she could be herself, silly at times, throwing snowballs at him like a three-year-old, rubbing the frozen snow on his leather jacket, remembering those paintings they would have enjoyed at the Louvre. And they would sail peacefully together, like Cleopatra in her barge, following the *berge* (riverbank) of the Seine. And lying down on a couch, free from a darker past like at a Passover Seder imitating the Romans, they would feed each other grapes from Solomon's vineyard.

New York
February 25, 2021

171

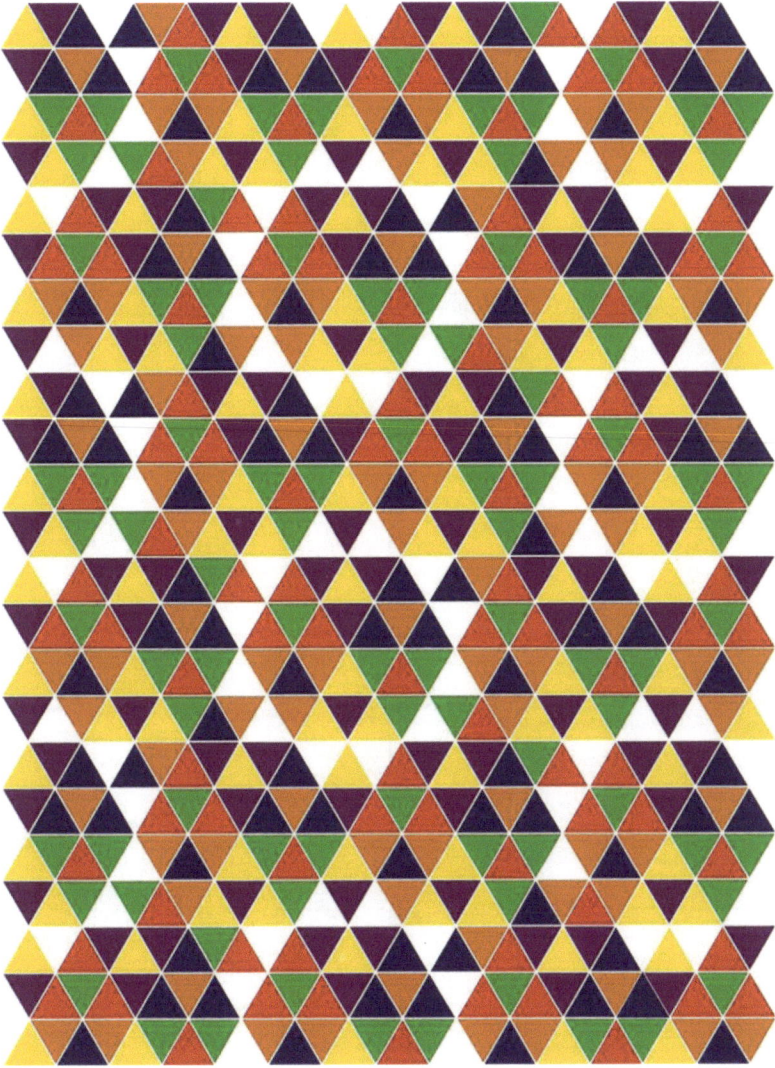

20 Deception

"You lied to me. I don't know any more what I should think about you. Don't be surprised if I do not respond to your messages."

Layla had pronounced those words only in her mind; nevertheless a tempest already shook the glass of her window, furiously thrusting its frigid wind into her living room through the slightly open window, as if the *djinns*, the malefic spirits, were trying to slip in.

Had she sent this note, it would have been a response, an opening wedge piercing a breach in her defense. The message would have invited a back and forth discussion and could have resumed their relationship. It disclosed her weakness and her struggle, her anger and her yearning, and it would render her more vulnerable than a stoic silence.

He had not just lied to her; he had robbed her of her most precious belongings, her youth, her trust, her passion, her body.

She had noticed him early during that international conference on geopolitics, which she attended as an intern of a prestigious consulting firm. She had observed him first – tall, slim, impeccably dressed in his classic, elegant dark suit with very discreet white stripes. He was talking comfortably to important lobbyists and to international policy makers. He seemed to know many of them personally and conducted animated and frank conversations in the hall leading to the

Grand Ballroom of the modern Washington hotel where the conference was organized.

She did not know yet that her firm had invited him to work as an advisor on the same topic which preoccupied her: The proxy war between Iran and Saudi Arabia, and the potential threat of an Iran-based Houthi insurgency in Yemen to international trade passing through the Bab-el-Mandeb straight, between the Arabian Peninsula and Djibouti. She was assigned to help him in his formulation of a policy position for lobbying the U.S. Government on behalf of the commercial clients of the firm.

She was seduced by his sharp analytical mind and by his knowledge of Washington politics. He needed her linguistic skills, and her knowledge of political science and religion, to navigate his way through sensitive Arabic and Iranian documents. At only 23, she was appreciated by the senior partners, and knew that she had brilliant prospects in the firm. In all modesty, few people were able to match her analytical ability. But he was. When he asked her to accompany him during his morning jogging, which included running up and down in circles on the many steps of the staircase leading to the Lincoln Memorial, she was also impressed with the determination and will expressed in his athletic body.

She could not resist when he invited her to l'Escargot, a fancy French restaurant in Washington, D.C., associated with the establishment of the same name in Paris, with its striking black wooden exterior and its intimate plush sitting. He barely needed to ask her out, because of the effect he had on her. An aura of assurance surrounded this enigmatic 40-year-old man (he had disclosed his age when she asked him over dinner) who, it turned out, would be so skilled at avoiding questions about his past that she almost suspected his consulting activities were a front. She fantasized that he had been, or was still involved, in a secret government agency which could not be named.

She had learned to live with his idiosyncrasies, and his extraordinary concerns for privacy. He was the last man she knew who still owned an old fashion flip phone to avoid being tracked, and who used a series of untraceable mail boxes and email addresses. She had been attracted by older men in the past, but never with such an age difference. It was a stretch for her; however she could see a future with their relationship growing into what would be a family.

It was a passionate affair, embracing body and mind, the brain and the soul. Eleven months had passed and the coals of passion were still burning hot. He had brought her not only to the original restaurant l'Escargot, rue Montorgueil in the former *Quartier des Halles* of Paris, but also to a secure semi-official meeting in the Kandahār Province of Afghanistan, held under heavy security, and to Saudi Arabia for a discussion with officials related to the ruling Prince.

One day, in an elegant hotel in New York, he was taking his morning shower after jogging in Central Park, and had left his pants on the chair by the secretary desk. It piqued her curiosity and she looked in his wallet at his driver's license. It was his name all right, but what she discovered made her freeze. She looked again in disbelief at the soft plasticized card. The birthdate was not of a 40-year-old man. He was 57.

She felt betrayed and stupidly naïve. Her hope for having found her dream guy, shattered. Who knows what other lies he had served up to her? She could not have children with a 57-year-old liar. She was so angry that she screamed at the steam coming out of the bathroom. "You lied to me! YOU LIED TO ME!" She couldn't pronounce anything else, lest the curse would unleash the *djinns* and cast a spell on him, and on her too. She wouldn't look at him ever again. She pictured his ageless face and body, as deceiving as his mind. She quickly grabbed her carry-on suitcase, her phone and her pocketbook, and rushed to leave the hotel room, abandoning him in the bathroom along with her toothbrush and the bottle of expensive perfume he had bought her. She ran through the hallway, the elevator, the hotel lobby, avoiding the inquisitive and surprised look on the concierge's face.

She never called him back or answered his messages. How selfish he was. He should have been dead to her. But three months later she had the urge to text him an explanation for her silence. But an explanation would have broken her silence, a silence she still wanted to maintain.

Instead of texting him, she decided to email him a short story with the word "Deception" in the subject line. She would use her literary skills to compose a fiction alluding to their life together. She would send the story as an attachment, with only the same word in the body of the email: "Deception," not even signing her name. And, to conceal her message further from him, the Master of Concealment, she would write partly in French, a language he did not know, forcing him, for spite, to have it translated. She promised herself to use French idioms and slang *à tire-larigot* (excessively), to fool a computerized translation program and force the software to make comical mistakes.

In her anger, and to make her story even more difficult to translate, she resolved to intersperse transliterated Persian words or even sentences, and to mix wide levels of language registers in French, from vile slang to elaborate and pretentious words, in the style of some Middle Eastern writers who juxtapose an elevated vocabulary, drawn from formal Arabic prose, with popular colloquial Arabic.

II

When Zaki learned about her deception, he severed all contacts with her, not knowing what to believe anymore. She misrepresented herself as ten years younger, and who knows which important detail she had forgotten to mention or had hidden from him? How could he trust any promise from her? When, in disbelief, he found an age associated with her on the internet, he initially brushed it off as a mistake. But then her reported birthdate was of the same zodiacal sign she had told him she was: Sagittarius. This reduced the odds of a mistake. The picture of herself she had provided was probably also ten years old. Although she looked younger than her age, he should have known. He would have accepted what was maybe the standard deduction of a year or two, but ten years!? She had not contacted him after he went silent. When the first holiday came, he texted her a brief greeting, in order to not be rude and break the possibility of a relationship. But when she followed up with a simple question, he did not answer, lest she would ask another question and try to renew the relationship too quickly.

He had liked her despite her lie. But then, if she appreciated him, why didn't she contact him earlier? She was playing to perfection the role of the woman, waiting for him to make his move according to stereotypical traditional roles. He would let her take the lead to ask him for dinner, or for a stroll in the park. He needed more time to digest her tale. He did not call her; until, under her spell, he decided to write her a fictional story, a story within a story, to share his torment with her. Not that he needed an apology, but at least he desired an acknowledgment, an understanding. However, the only words which came out of his pain spoke of his reminiscence of his enthusiasm during their first encounter.

Clenching his pen in distress, he looked at his manuscript and at his failed attempt to draw empathy from her:

Déception

"Sur les chapeaux de roue", c'est comment il aurait pu décrire leur première rencontre. Certes, il avait succombé aux filets charmeurs de la damoiselle qui, telle une araignée de mer, avait tissé ses mailles pour attraper le poisson. La charmeuse de Parme, s'était parée, non d'une chartreuse, mais d'une longue paire de bottes noires remontant au-dessus des genoux et laissant apparaitre furtivement sous sa jupe, la ligne blanche du bas de ses cuisses, nues malgré le froid glacial. "Je n'aime pas mettre des collants" avait-elle déclaré, la coquine. Déception mitigée par son absence de réponse quant à savoir si elle eût été disposée à surmonter son inconfort pour lui plaire, silence qu'il prit pour un oui préliminaire et tentateur. Mettant bas son masque révélant un sourire trompeusement naïf, la gonzesse se laissa tripoter les mains lorsqu'ils s'assirent au café du musée, elle admirant le postérieur de la statue musclée d'un guerrier vu de dos en tenue d'Adam avant la faute, et lui louchant subrepticement sur les plus lointaines demoiselles de marbres aux pauses souples et relaxées, elles aussi en tenues plus que légères.[30]

---

[30] **Gibberish Translation, by Google Translate:**

Disappointment

"On top of the wheel" [**Note from Layla:** *"Off to a flying start" would have been a more accurate translation of the French idiom.*] is how he might have described their first meeting. Certainly, he had succumbed to the charming nets of the damsel who, like a spider crab, had woven its meshes to catch the fish. The charmeuse of Parma, was adorned, not in a chartreuse, but in a long pair of black boots going up above the knees and letting appear furtively under her skirt, the white line of the bottom of her thighs, naked in spite of freezing cold. "I don't like to wear pantyhose," the naughty said. Mixed disappointment at her lack of response as to whether she would have been willing to overcome her discomfort to please him, a silence he took for a preliminary and tempting yes. Putting

The higher the crush on the young damsel, the more painful the crash when he awoke to a lady older than him. Although their difference in age could have been acceptable had it been announced upfront, the deception had torn his enthusiasm.

III

With a sigh of relief, Layla pressed SEND to deliver him her missive about Zaki. He had betrayed her much more than Zaki had in her story; but he maybe would relate to Zaki's character and realize how his deception unleashed the demons wounding her.

New York
February 28, 2020

---

down her mask revealing a deceptively naive smile, the chick let her hands fiddle with as they sat down at the museum cafe, admiring the posterior of the muscular statue of a warrior seen from behind in Adam's outfit before the fault, and squinting him surreptitiously on the most distant marble maidens with supple and relaxed pauses, also in more than light outfits.

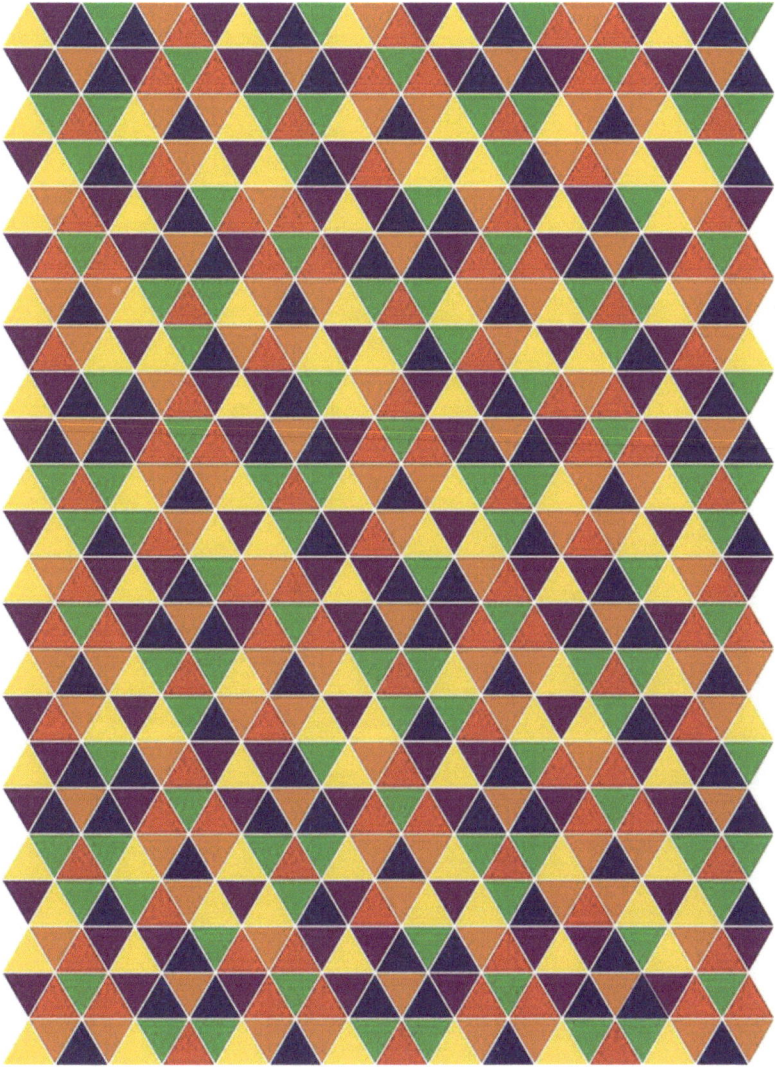

21 The Storyteller

Zaki knew he just had the time to slide delicately down the couch with a loud moan and lie down on the floor. He had barely enough energy to place his body on the hard carpet in the least uncomfortable position without crushing his glasses, as a computer shutting down unexpectedly would use its last drop of power to close the open programs and make an emergency backup of the unsaved files, passing through a state between awake and asleep, like that same evening when he fell asleep still talking with a friend and woke up when he heard what nonsense he had just uttered, realizing he had just been asleep for a second. Zaki was this kind of writer who would embark blindly on a journey, writing without any map or plan, curious to discover what would happen to his characters, like a barque without sails or oars is tossed haphazardly from one bank to another by the strong current of a narrow river. He would try to remember what brilliant ideas, and brilliant they certainly appeared to him then, were created during this in-between state, half dreaming, half-consciously thinking of his characters. When he had recharged his battery, like the computer waking up from its sleep mode, he would feverishly try to recover the lost data from a smart dialogue or gripping scene. Piece by piece, Zaki would attempt to weave this data into the text. But the recovered pieces where incoherent, and would not blend in smoothly with the rest of the story, and they stuck out like starchy lumps in a sauce. Zaki learned that he could sometimes control which language he used when he was in shutting down mode. But he was surprised to discover that the form, the language he chose, took control of the content. When he tried to write a story in French, he could not follow the stream of the English narrative where that French story was embedded. By switching languages, Zaki's references had also changed and instead of a gracious flow between the two languages, there was a gap or an abrupt cascade, from pensive and introspective, to gaudy and flirtatious.

Why was Zaki still writing stories, when he knew they were failing him in his wish to connect, comfort, explain, share, or persuade. His stories were falling flat, loudly and painfully as a belly flop. In his last piece, *Déception*, a story in French within an English story called *Deception*, he couldn't relate to Layla. Worse, she could even have found his words insulting, objectifying, the opposite of his intention. Of course, she would not respond. When he wrote *A Thousand Camels for your Gazelle,* he expected Layla to appreciate his compassion for her suffering. Why did he choose Layla again as the name of this older and very different character? By laziness, or because all women merged into the archetype "THE woman," a woman he yearned for but failed to understand? She too hadn't answered him. And when Zaki wrote *A Loud Inaudible Bang,* he—was it Zaki?—was aware that he had crossed the line with his stories about her. Did he have the chutzpah to send her that story by snail mail in a fancy envelope, intruding a second time? I don't think he meant to be so insensitive. If he had sent it, of course she would not have responded, what would he have expected? When he wrote *"ONE": The Story of Malka Risze,* who was he trying to impress? Himself or his colleagues? Or with *Hallelujah,* was he hoping to engage Lena, an impressive writer who had composed in a few minutes a story about a woman in despair, story which haunted him for weeks. Was he tempted to intrude again and ask her by email for a copy of her hopeless story? Of course he was; but did he press SEND to that email? I hope not. I hope he learned from his mistakes. A mistake which could have been repeated had he—but was it still the same Zaki?—sent *The Blessing of the Hands* to his innocent co-worker in the I.T. department, who stirred her oil and touched him without any physical contact. If he had the foolishness to have sent her that story, I hope that she

186

would have mercifully ignored this breach of boundaries. Or when he wrote *The Day After the Plague*, or *Gourmandize* or some other stories in this book, whom was he trying to relate to or seduce? What was the need for those stories?

This time, Zaki decided to write a story which would impress no one, relate to no one, maybe his darkest story which he had no intention to share. He decided to finally write a story about breaching boundaries. And this was Zaki's next story: *Boundaries*.

New York
March 9, 2021

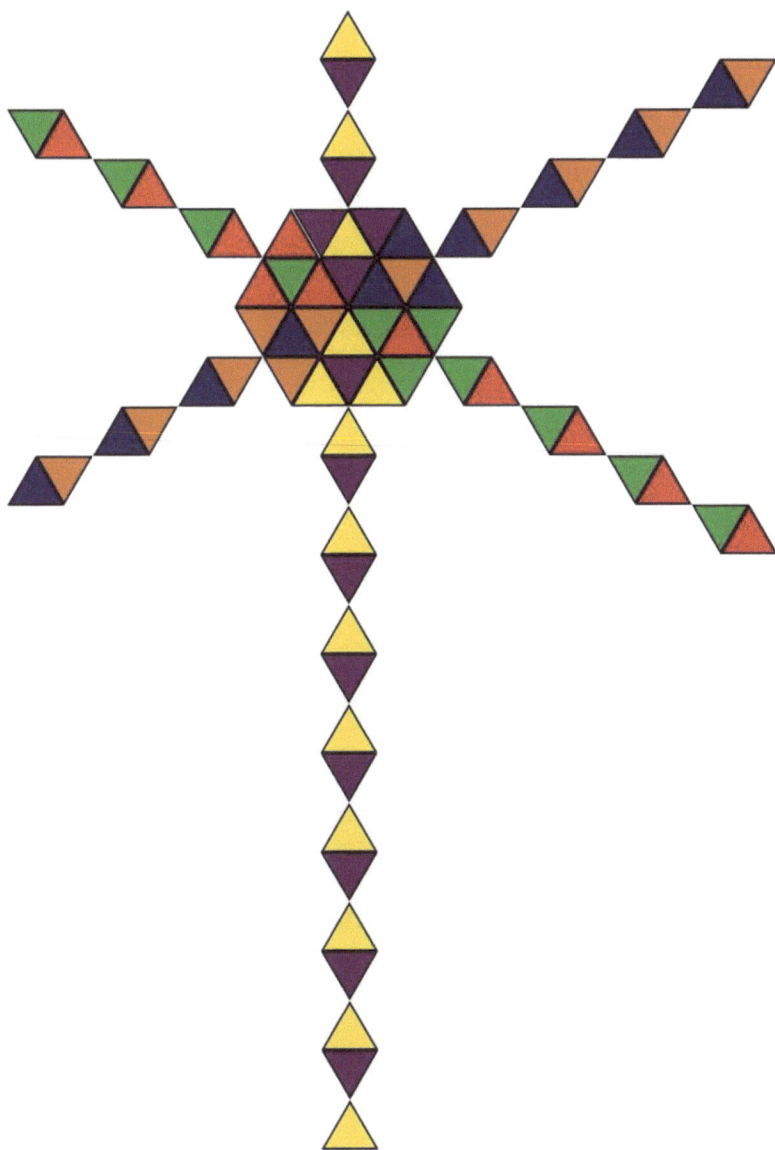

22 Boundaries

Adina pinched her lips in her own very peculiar way, when Isabelle resurfaced. Zaki knew that soon, dark dimples would mark Adina's rosy cheeks, and that her eyes would become humid and then wet. Adina was possessed by the spirit of Isabelle, a ten-year-old little girl. Adina was a tall attractive thirty-year-old woman with long, silky black hair, who worked for an important hospital system, assisting Ben, her supervisor, in his administrative responsibilities. She had just learned of her acceptance to a Master's Program in Public Administration in Health Care Management at a prestigious university. It was a real achievement for her and the next step for her career in her chosen field.

Zaki, her supportive husband, congratulated Adina on her success. It was a moment to savor. A year ago Ben had been considerate with her. He invited her to a fancy leadership weekend retreat. Then, the hospital administration switched to working mostly remotely, like most businesses in New York. Ben would email her or text her day and night, even during the weekends, as if working from home dissolved temporal boundaries. Adina couldn't argue because she didn't want to be laid off – many of her colleagues had been. Ben had refused to promote her, the way he had promoted others. It was as if he wanted her to stay close, dependent on him, with no chance of growing on her own.

Isabelle was silent at home and in school. She was a good child, not making waves, always doing her homework assiduously. She had no one to confide in. At home, mother did all the talking, unburdening herself to Isabelle. She went over her marital problems with her daughter, even asking for Isabelle's advice: Should she divorce father?

But Isabelle stayed silent. Silent with father too, and keeping his confidence, when she discovered he had an affair and he asked her to say nothing. She would listen to all of mother's loneliness, whether mother was drunk or sober. Isabelle was afraid to say anything which would break the family, and leave her alone in the streets. What would she, a ten-year-old girl, do if her parents abandoned her? Mother did not seem aware of her little girl's feelings, and was just flooding Isabelle with her own adult anxiety, not realizing how terrorizing this would be for her child. And father was no help. He would not have kept her if her parents divorced.

So Isabelle stayed silent. She could speak all right. But her aim was to avoid calling attention to herself, as if her silence could keep everything as it was.

For many years Isabelle dreamed about doors. Doors opened or ajar, or not closed very well, leaving her exposed to intruders. Doors she would try and fail to shut. Door. Doors. Or even a hole in the wall. But she also had happy dreams. Dreams so real that for a while she thought it was possible to rise and fly through the air standing up. In her dreams, she had learned how to control her flight with her body, up or down, right or left. She was a free spirit and would discover countryside, mountains, cities, during flights so gripping that she would regret waking up. Waking up was a reprieve after the scary door dreams.

Isabelle was silently observing Adina's success while everyone congratulated her on her achievement. Isabelle, the silent one, uttered a few words, *You don't deserve it.* When Adina thought of announcing her departure to her boss, Isabelle became nervous and screamed, *Don't say anything.* Isabelle could not bear breaking up the office. For her, the office was the family. Even if Ben ended up violating boundaries by calling her any time, day or night, after the

192

office started to work remotely. Adina's boss had valued her before. He had invited her to that leadership retreat. He had given her the attention that parents provide when they take care of their child, the kind of attention Isabelle never got from her parents.

Isabelle had learned to stay silent for survival. She did not tell her parents about the "friend of the family" (mainly of her father), who took advantage of her for years. She saw him as a poor lonely soul. When mother asked her, after being alerted by an aunt who reported sexual abuse to her children from that 'friend of the family,' if he had done anything inappropriate, Isabelle denied it. *Don't talk. Don't hurt him. Don't upset the family. A few words from me could change everything, break the family apart and I would end up alone out in the streets.*

To reduce the anguish, Isabelle learned to detach herself from what he would do to her, as if she was not even aware of his touching. "Consenting victim," this is what she called herself. Once, when a little older, she heard him knock at the locked door of her apartment. He was so lonely, so desperate. She did not have the heart to hurt him. How could she? *He pays attention to me. He has been nice, sometimes.* So she opened the door, knowing perfectly what would happen. *I am disgusting, a whore, a tramp.* Her body repulsed her.

Adina adopted an abandoned dog that had been rescued by the animal shelter, a mixed-breed, clearly with some Cocker Spaniel, with her lustrous brown-red fur. She was an affectionate and demonstrative dog. Adina took good care of her and gave her a loving home in the country house. They would go outside in the grass and play catch with a stick. They would cuddle with each other on the couch. But then the dog got really sick. She was vomiting on the sofa for weeks. Zaki wanted to return her to the shelter but Isabelle shrieked: *Abandon the dog to the animal shelter?? No. No, you cannot do that to her.* Adina recalled that as a little girl, Isabelle's age, her parents gave her a puppy dog for her birthday. Adina named her "Kelev." The puppy was her best friend, her only friend and confidant, and she, the silent one, would talk to Kelev for hours. Kelev would listen with her big puppy dog eyes and raised eyebrows, looking intently at Adina, sometimes licking the face of the little girl, to wipe her sorrow away and comfort her. But the puppy dog became ill, moaning all night, obviously in pain, and losing weight. One day Kelev disappeared. "Where is my friend?" Adina had asked her father. "I returned the dog to the pet store," was his response. And she believed him for a whole year, until she discovered the puppy's pink leash tucked in deep inside the trunk of the car. "Why didn't you return Kelev with her leash?" little Adina asked her father? Adina still remembered her father laughing so loudly and for so long that she had to put her hands over her ears. "Did you really believe I returned your dog to the pet store? Of course not. I abandoned it on the sidewalk, jumped in the car and took off. How funny it was to see it running after the car with its little legs!"

This puppy dog was me, said Isabelle. *If I complain or even say something, I too could be abandoned any time, like my puppy dog.* DON'T ABANDON THE DOG. DON'T SEND HER BACK TO THE ANIMAL SHELTER.

Adina had learned to live with Isabelle, the little girl she had been twenty years ago, the little girl still haunting her. For a long time, she took Isabelle's voice as her own. But then, with time, she realized that she was being possessed by the little girl she had been and somehow still was. Adina learned to separate herself from Isabelle, first to acknowledge her, and then to nurture her. But Isabelle refused all attention because she did not deserve it. So Adina let Isabelle talk. Isabelle would break her silence when she felt she was in a dangerous situation, or when Adina was using Isabelle's body for disgusting repulsive acts with Zaki. This interfered with

Adina's love life. Adina listened to Isabelle's words like nobody had listened before, except for Kelev, giving Isabelle time, soothing the little girl, and massaging her shoulders and arms with a lavender hydrating lotion, singing her lullabies, or asking her about the flights, the countries she had explored from above, and about her joy.

New York
April 8, 2021

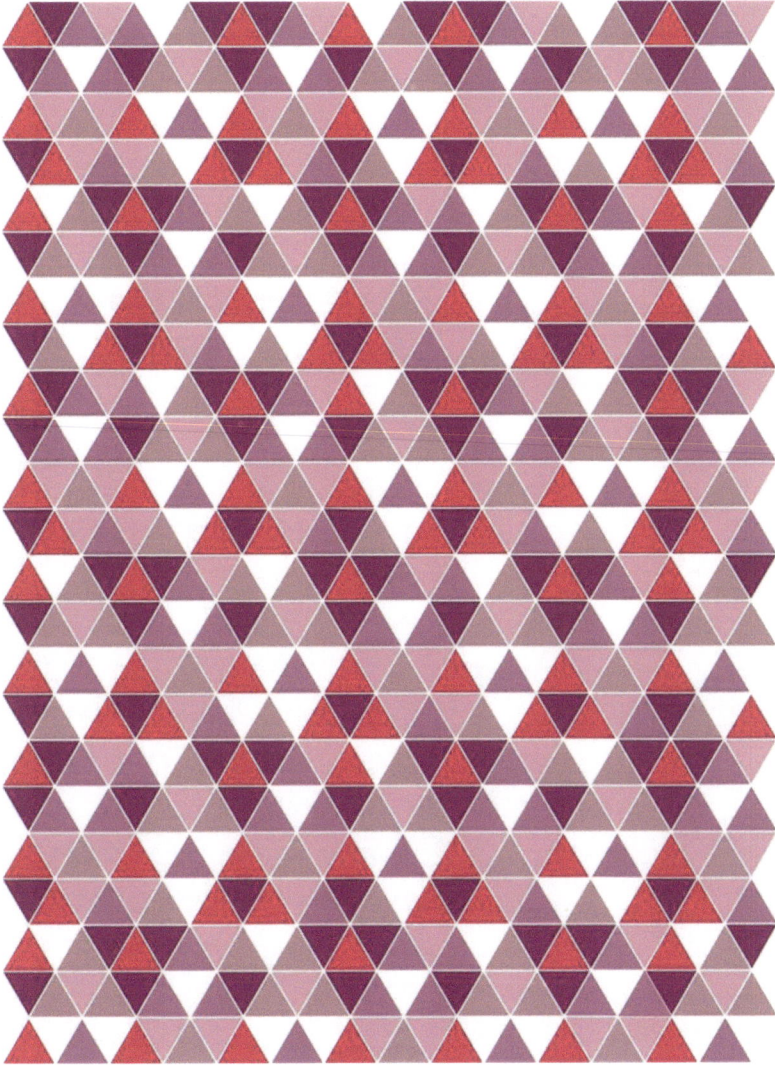

23 Triangles

The fuzzy edges of the bright yellow horizontal line merged with the boundary of the dark purple-blue square shapes above and below the line. Dina surrounded herself with those colors. On her sides and even her back, she could sense the four paintings she had seen two years before in that small, square magical room at the Yale University Art Gallery. She floated between the colors, absorbed in a trance, her small frame transported across the ocean to an even deeper experience inside large oval rooms, submerged in the vibrations of Monet's Water Lilies at the Musée de l'Orangerie in Paris.
Why was she here?

Yellow. Purple-blue... Did Rothko combine random colors with no meaning, hoping that others would give them a brilliant interpretation?
What was she doing here?

"I see you like the painting."

Who was he? Yes. Rosner. What does he want from me? To judge me? With his deceptively gentle voice?

Dina remembered the voice. That fine gravelly voice, its soft smoky bass, like a commentator on the radio, its authoritative and reassuring tone, not the hoarse voice of a jazz singer, à la Louis Armstrong. But still attractive, seductive. She had loved this virile voice, a voice just like this, when she was still inexperienced, barely out of her French high school. It was during her summer romance with François, a tall thin boy her age. François had brought her to a small fishing town in Normandy, surrounded by its famous cliffs. There he had

199

driven her up a twisting road, climbing along a cliff. And he, as inexperienced at driving as she was in love, had lost control of the small car which spun around like a four-sided dreidel in the center of a curve, and she had looked, calm and mesmerized, through the big windshield as if absorbed in a movie with its dream-like flow of scenery racing by. The triangular street sign bordered with red, warning of a *virage dangereux* (dangerous curve), flashed in her eyes as a straight line of red triangles. But the car did not tumble across the middle of the deserted road or crash into a tree. They had lost touch after a year, but they reconnected when François had called her from France three months ago, and, after fifteen years, without even seeing him, she had fallen all over again for that husky voice, the distance of time and place dissolving.

"My name, again, is Doctor Rosner. I will be your doctor while you are here. Could you tell me your name?" The man was devilishly polite, with his white coat and shirt, and his tie with its pattern of flashy blue triangles. *I should have known he'd wear this tie on purpose.* He had fine silver metal glasses above his pale peach, duck-shaped mask, behind a clear plastic shield that covered his entire face.

Dina's long brown hair covered her eyes, conveniently hiding her much better than the doctor's face shield protected him. It was annoying to breathe through her white mask, but it shielded her not only from infections but also from Rosner's nosey eyes. She turned her head rapidly and all she could see was the line of blue triangles from his tie, and this time it fell more dangerously than the red triangular warning sign on the street in Normandy. She imagined the equivalent sign here in New York State, two yellow triangles joined to form a tilted square.

Already in her *chambre de bonne*, a little room under the roof, in Paris when she was a young student at the École des

Beaux-Arts, she designed an elaborate pattern of triangles, with each triangle filled with only one of the six main colors of the rainbow.

"I see that you don't want to talk," said Rosner. "Maybe you would like to write instead?" And he gave her a nice blank piece of paper and a pen.

Dina, who had been motionless till then, was as mesmerized by this tempting white page as by his enticing voice and couldn't resist grabbing the pen. She did not write a word; she drew. She drew triangles, a full page of triangles. *Too bad if this Rosner thinks I am crazy for drawing triangles. I need to.* Dina silently drew identical triangles with the concentration of a monk meticulously composing an intricate sand mandala.

"Would you like some crayons to put some color into your drawing?"

How did he know? He knew. He had known when he put on the blue triangle tie. She would draw most of the blue color last, after she had used the other five colors. She guessed that he would recognize the complex pattern, even if he could not duplicate it exactly.

Dina started by coloring a rainbow circle made of six equal triangles. From there she ran an arrow of red triangles in a line which joined another rainbow hub. She continued connecting the hubs with aligned arrows of triangles in complementary colors. She replicated the complex multicolored pattern, over and over, with concentration, almost in a trance, as if repeating a mantra. And then, between the lines connecting the hubs, she would fill the blank space with more triangles, forming secondary rainbow circles with adjacent complementary colors.

How long had she been drawing? She couldn't tell. Rosner must have left a long time ago.

Who sent her to the hospital? How did she get here?

It was a mistake. She would show Rosner her true colorful drawing and he would understand that she had all her marbles, and he would release her. François would show up and explain who she was, and he would take her away from this place, and they would live happily ever after.

New York,
May 31, 2021

Triangles and Squares, photo by Daniel Rosen, 1993

Afterword

By William S. Cohen

This collection of stories addresses a varied range of human relationships. The relationships in the stories are not only between humans, of course, but also with words (as in ***Verbal Jousting***, in ***Colorful Words*** or in ***Stone-Words***), with God, "The Master of the Words" in ***Morning Blessing***, and with ancestors (***Ancestral Merit***).

The stories give a voice to a grandiose woman in ***Hallelujah*** and to an abused little girl in ***Boundaries***. Such first person (***Hallelujah***) or close third person narratives, as in ***"ONE": The Story of Malka Risze***, can allow therapists to enter a patient's experience through their own intimate view of the world without utilizing the usual medical jargon. In that last story, the narrative itself is used as a therapeutic tool to master an anticipated trauma.

Ultimately, the relationships are also with the stories themselves, as a means to connect with others. A story may be all that remains to us. A story replacing a lost heirloom in ***Ancestral Merit****: All that Tom could pass on was a story. A story of elegant watches, which were not completely lost since they lived on in memory*. The story can be about an unwritten story, as in ***Colorful Words****: All that was left was the story. The story of a missed story. A misstory. A mystery*. The story preserves the memory of an Arab shopkeeper's act of kindness toward a stranger in ***A Thousand Camels for Your Gazelle***. Story can also have the power to ease the fear of losing a necessary ritual. The story itself can replace a therapeutic religious ritual, as in ***"ONE": The Story of Malka Risze***.

The theme of a story being an integral part of another story is present in the form of a letter within the story of *A Loud Inaudible Bang*, and later on in *Deception*. Sometimes, a story gives birth to another story and the boundary between the two may be fuzzy. The blurring between text and footnote in *Morning Blessing*, where the first footnote becomes, progressively, a part of the main text, is an example, in the external form of the layout of the printed page, of crossing boundaries.

The boundary between being a character in a story and being a storyteller emerges toward the end of this collection in the person of Zaki. In *Deception*, Zaki is a storyteller, or at least he tries to be. In *The Storyteller*, Zaki's role becomes enlarged, more defined. In a way, that story is a story about the stories crossing boundaries in this book. In this story introducing *Boundaries*, the character of Zaki himself crosses boundaries from a fictional character written by Layla, in *Deception*, into a character who is himself an author, a storyteller. In *Morning Prayer*, and maybe also in *Maya*, according to one possible interpretation suggested in *Verbal Jousting*, the boundaries between gender is blurred reflecting an androgynous (or non-binary) God.

The stories are often about words and about our ambiguous relationship with language. Plays with words abound through those stories, often across languages. In *Gourmandize*, the play with words sounding alike – *les frissons/les fruits sont* (thrill/the fruits are) – is untranslatable. The play can be deceptively hidden in a French *accent aigu* (acute accent) on the letter "*e*." In *Deception*, *Déception* is a small French story embedded in a larger story in English. However both words are *faux-amis* (false cognates), as *déception* in French does not mean "deception" but "disappointment." In that story, Laya created the character Zaki, and she writes in French as an act of war and vengeful deception against her deceiving lover. The opacity of the language, written on

206

purpose to be concealing and difficult to translate, is written in anger as revenge against the lover she abandons ("The Master of Concealment") and who most likely would struggle to understand any clues from her.

The theme of concealment is also found in **Concealed**, where a secular painting and a Biblical text are juxtaposed to address the concealment of sexuality. In **Maya**, the dressing up reveals a stormy sexuality which had been concealed up to this point. Later on, **Verbal Jousting** revisits the story of **Maya** and discusses a revision of the text *when the main protagonist was now concealed (or revealed?)*. Here, the story **Maya** becomes the subject of another story. The academic commentary on **"ONE": The Story of Malka Risze** notes that the narrator's voice in the story is in the close third person, and that it could be a literary fiction from an author with a different biographical background: "The power of fiction allows this revealing through concealment. I could not have written about such a powerful fear in the first person."

Although each story in this book can be read independently, they interconnect as a whole and, as in **Verbal Jousting**, one story can fill in the blanks left by another, inviting the reader to reinterpret the text. As Owen Lewis commented on Doctor Rosen's previous book, *Butterfly Words: Relationships, A Psychiatrist's Narrative*[31]:

> **While parts of the "story" are explicit, other parts are omitted, and in a sense, the reader is asked to become psychiatrist to this psychiatrist/writer, to**

---

[31] Rosen, Daniel: *Butterfly Words: Relationships, A Psychiatrist's Narrative.* International Psychoanalytic Books, New York, NY. 2019.
Comments by: Owen Lewis, author of *Sometimes Full of Daylight*
Clinical Professor of Psychiatry at Columbia University
2016 Hippocrates Prize for Poetry and Medicine

engage with what's said, to speculate about the unsaid.

Words are analyzed, compared, commented, and two texts are just plain Bible commentaries: ***Looking for Paradise*** and ***The Binding of Isaac***, although they could be seen as a development of the bible study in ***Ancestral Merit***. Throughout many stories, words are translated mainly from French or Hebrew. We find a liberal use of the Hebrew Bible and of various Jewish religious texts. Occasionally there is a mention of Arabic in ***Morning Blessing*** and ***A Thousand Camels for Your Gazelle*** and of Greek in ***The Blessing of the Hands***.

The cultural settings of the stories are various. Most of the religious references are Jewish, but some are drawn from Christian, Muslim or Buddhist traditions, rituals or mythology. As in *Butterfly Words*, this collection of writings merges religious and secular themes and references, expresses optimism and despair, yearning and distancing, detachment and closeness, love and death, and has us travel through stones and sparks, letters and spirits, smoke and smile, songs and cries, east and west, hidden and revealed.

About the author

If you really want to know... but I don't feel like going into it. All I can tell you is about that book I loved as a child. I must have read it a thousand times, no kidding. I did not know English then, so I read it in French: "L'Attrape Cœurs," it was called. I could not find my copy of it when I finally moved all my stuff from storage in Paris. I don't know what happened to the book. It was a pretty important book for me, this boy lost in New York, wondering where the ducks in Central Park went in the freezing winter. Even now, I can't figure it out. Maybe you know? And when he fell in love with a young nun in a long dress and a blue marine sweater. Maybe it's not exactly like that in the book. I lost the book – okay? But it was something like that. No, you don't have to be a nun and all, but I remember that one who was so nice with a visibly challenged guy at the Jewish Museum. I did not talk to her then, it was many years ago, and she was not a nun. So, you see, you don't have to be a nun. I never said you did.

www.ingramcontent.com/pod-product-compliance
Lightning Source LLC
Chambersburg PA
CBHW040936030426
42335CB00001B/2